Collectable Names and Designs in Women's Shoes

For all those that appreciate shoes as an art form.

Collectable Names and Designs in Women's Shoes

Tracy Martin

WHITE
OWL

First published in Great Britain in 2018 by
Pen & Sword White Owl
an imprint of
Pen & Sword Books Ltd
47 Church Street
Barnsley
South Yorkshire
S70 2AS

ISBN 978 1 78159 785 9

A CIP catalogue record for this book is available from the British Library

Typeset in Ehrhardt by
Mac Style Ltd, Bridlington, East Yorkshire
Printed and bound in India by
Replika Press Pvt. Ltd.

Pen & Sword Books Limited incorporates the imprints of Atlas,
Archaeology, Aviation, Discovery, Family History, Fiction, History, Maritime,
Military, Military Classics, Politics, Select, Transport, True Crime, Air World,
Frontline Publishing, Leo Cooper, Remember When, Seaforth Publishing,
The Praetorian Press, Wharncliffe Local History, Wharncliffe Transport,
Wharncliffe True Crime and White Owl.

For a complete list of Pen & Sword titles please contact
PEN & SWORD BOOKS LIMITED
47 Church Street, Barnsley, South Yorkshire, S70 2AS, England
E-mail: enquiries@pen-and-sword.co.uk
Website: www.pen-and-sword.co.uk

Contents

Foreword

My fascination with shoes began the moment I created my first pair of high heels. Aged just six years old I glued wooden cotton reels onto cardboard soles and then attached them to my feet with rubber bands. Balancing precariously on my improvised footwear, I was thrilled to be rewarded for my efforts by being given a pair of pink plastic glitter mules which I loved to bits. My future career as a shoe designer was unwittingly endorsed.

The next pair of shoes I remember with great affection was a pair of iconic chunky early 1970s high-heeled platforms in green glitter fabric (I have a penchant for glitter). Worn almost threadbare and now forty years on they still reside in a battered box under my wardrobe holding fond memories for me. These shoes were the catalyst for my career as, soon after buying these wonderfully impractical and exuberant platforms, I felt inspired to design and make my own theatrical shoe statements.

The 1970s was an extraordinary decade of youthful self-discovery and of almost unbridled self-expression and individuality. There was a desire to shock which, combined with a mood of playful fun, unleashed a flowering of British talent and eccentricity. Living in London at the time, I was fortunate enough to find a master shoemaker to teach me the skills of bespoke shoe making through which I was able to find my own path of self-expression. It was very much a personal exploration and I had no 'market' in mind. I would wear my new creations to themed parties organized by friends in the fashion world, and when I received an ecstatic response to my designs and was showered with requests for shoes, it struck me I had found my career.

Today, I am still inspired by themes and love the challenge of translating these ideas into footwear. Shoes are so much more than functional forms or whimsical decoration; across all countries and cultures they have a special significance and allure. Topping wish lists worldwide, regardless of practicability, high-heeled shoes are desired for the wonderful emotional uplift they bestow.

Designing shoes has become my life and so I was extremely flattered when asked by the delightful Tracy Martin if I would write the foreword to her book *Collectable Names and Designs in Women's Shoes*. Tracy has a passion for design, creativity and innovation which is evident throughout the pages as she explores the social history behind footwear designs, providing a colourful insight into the evolution of the shoe from Ancient Egyptian sandals to the present day. Tracy explains how certain styles have gone full circle whilst others form groundbreaking contemporary fashion statements placing a spotlight on those styles which she feels have star potential.

Merging the boundaries between fashion and the arts is an area that Tracy also focuses on. She has handpicked her own personal favourite shoe designers who she believes not only create wonderful wearable footwear but also use the simple form of a shoe to produce sculptural works of art.

This book is a world away from just a picture book of shoes. It opens our eyes to the richness and variety of footwear, and gives us a much deeper understanding and appreciation of what footwear is all about.

It has been a real pleasure to share my own passion for shoes with Tracy. Her enthusiasm is so infectious that you cannot help but fall in love with footwear, not only as functional necessities but also as amazing achievements of craftsmanship and design that continue to astonish, delight and amuse.

Thea Cadabra, Shoe Designer

Thea Cadabra's *All Weather* shoe, 1978.

Introduction

Shoes are my passion! I just can't help myself, they call to me and I have to own them. Enticed by the outrageous designs, extrovert styles and rich embellishments – they are my biggest fashion weakness.

For me, they are not simply a necessity for protecting the feet, and comfort certainly doesn't come into it. My shoes need to get noticed. I want people to stare with envy as I, proud as a peacock, showcase the works of art that adorn my feet. A twenty-first century status symbol, shoes have, in my opinion, replaced diamonds as being a girl's best friend.

So when I was asked to write this book *Collectable Names and Designs in Women's Shoes* you can appreciate how I jumped at the chance. A dream job, indulging my passion, spending days surrounded by images and information on fantastic footwear and even buying the odd pair, in the name of research, of course!

Suddenly I was catapulted into shoe heaven as I began to explore the social history of shoes, the individual designers and their creations as well as the inspiration behind the designs. This book also, as the title suggests, focuses on the collectability of footwear so, in my role as a fashion collectables expert, I will consider why shoes have become so desirable in collectors' circles. I will be cherry picking my own personal favourites, sharing my knowledge on what to look out for and giving tips on where to buy and which of the iconic vintage designs to snap up. For example, 1920s bar shoes, 1960s Go-go boots, chunky glam rock platforms dating from the 1970s and Vivienne Westwood's 1980s Pirate boots have all become groundbreaking designs which have contributed to the ever-changing face of fashion.

The social history of footwear is also an integral part of shoe collecting as shoes can epitomise an era, bringing back nostalgic memories and recalling the music, film and social scenes of the decade in which they appeared. I will be pointing out which decades influenced specific designs, how society has made an impression on the development of shoes and singling out key designs that have become the 'holy grail' for collectors.

Another avenue I have decided to explore is that of shoes as an art form. With designers constantly pushing the boundaries by re-working traditional designs and adding their own unique contemporary twists, many shoes have become artistic works of art that wouldn't look out of place on show in an exhibition installation. So I have decided to also look at footwear that represents incredible feats of craftsmanship. Some pairs even the most dedicated *fashionista* would be unable to wear whilst others are so extreme that only

1970s red patent platform shoe.

the most fashion forward would possess enough confidence to strut down the street in them. These undisputed works of art demonstrate the impact the simple form of a shoe has had on the much wider world of sculptural artistry.

I guarantee that as you read *Collectable Names and Designs in Women's Shoes* you will begin to look at shoes with fresh eyes as you gasp at the styles and have your breath taken away by the designs. Crammed with information and images of innovative, sculptural and outrageous footwear, this book celebrates the shoe as a collectable work of art whilst examining the social history and progressive journey of footwear.

The ultimate style-savvy companion, this book is for those that appreciate heels as an artform and feel the need to satisfy their inner shoe fetish. If that's you, I hope you enjoy reading *Collectable Names and Designs in Women's Shoes* as much as I enjoyed writing it.

Omar Angel Perez *Emmanuelle Zipper Front* stiletto.

Chapter 1

Collecting Shoes

'*I did not have three thousand pairs of shoes, I had one thousand and sixty*'.

Imelda Marcos, former First Lady of the Philippines

Many of you ladies have probably never even considered that all of those pairs of shoes stacked high in your wardrobe, thrown under the bed or scattered around the house could be classed as valuable collectables. However, there is a possibility that one or two of your prized pairs could be eagerly sought by collectors.

When it comes to the collectability of shoes there are various avenues to explore. Many people choose to concentrate on acquiring antique pairs with the elaborately decorated examples being the most desirable. Others prefer to amass shoes dating from the twentieth century onwards, sometimes dedicating their collection to just one particular decade or a specific style, such as 1970s platforms or 1960s court shoes. However, a more recent trend is for snapping up the newest designer and high street offerings in the hope that these twenty first century shoes will eventually become must-haves on the collectors market.

It doesn't really matter which option you choose as all areas are already demonstrating buoyancy but I will stress that the whole point to collecting shoes is that they bring enjoyment and, of course, are heels that you instantly fall in love with. I personally own an eclectic mix of styles, decades and designers which I have purchased because I couldn't bear the thought of living without them! I do wear all my heels (all right, I confess to only wearing the expensive pairs on carpet and not in the street) and gain great pleasure when someone exclaims 'Wow I love your shoes!' They are indeed a thing of beauty and it is with this thought in mind that you should be purchasing those heels that you truly must have, no matter what. It is only then, as you start to buy the odd pair here and there, that you come to realise you have amassed quite a collection.

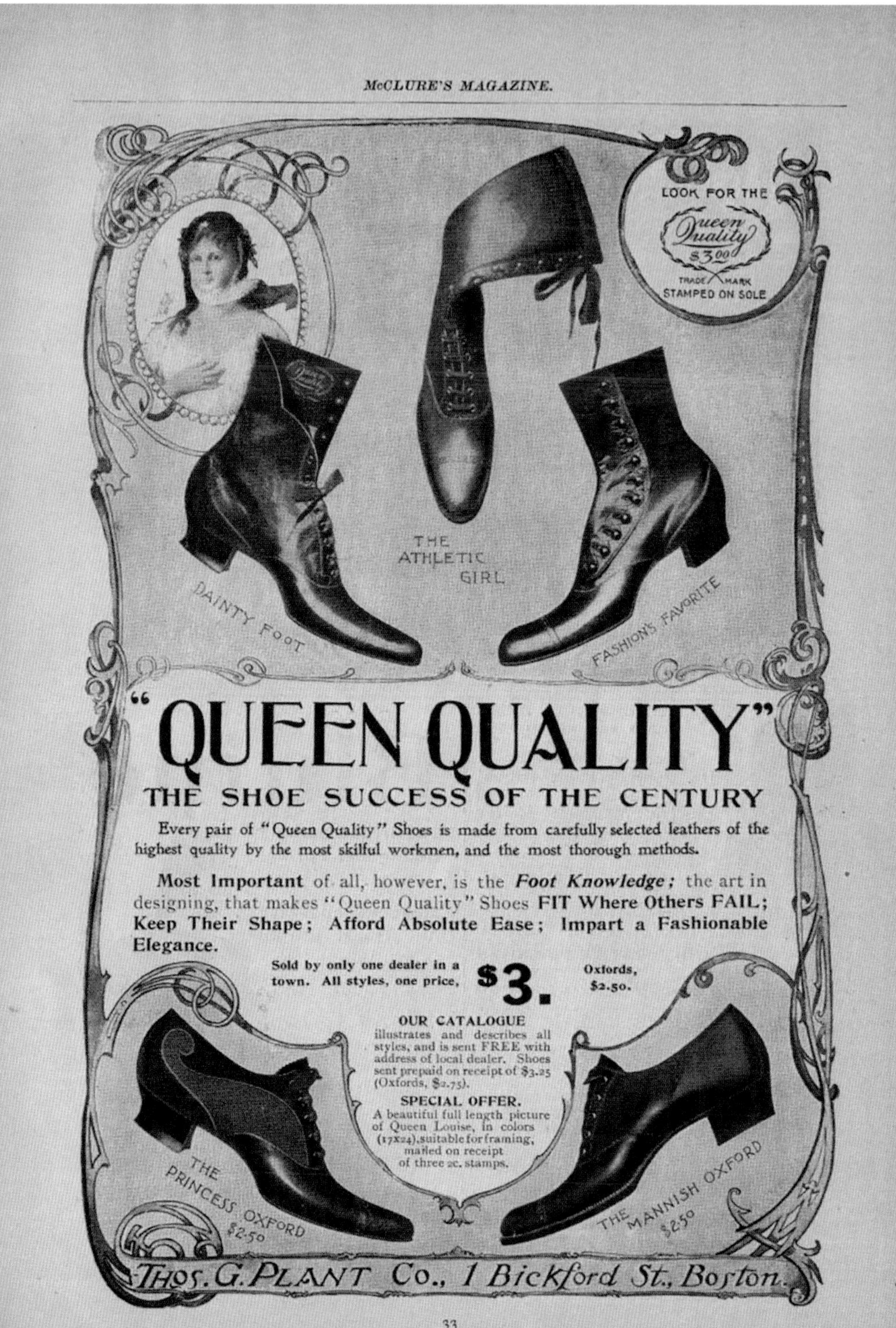

1899 magazine advertisement for 'Queen Quality' shoes.

Collecting antique and early twentieth century shoes

Many antique shoes are housed in museums around the world so that is why, when great examples dating to the early centuries come up for sale, you are not only competing with other avid collectors but also with museums. Even shoes dating to the Victorian era are getting scarce, with the button boot proving the most popular due to its recent fashion revival. People wish to own the original examples where possible as they appreciate the importance of wearing a true piece of history on their feet.

Genuine Victorian *button boots* made of satin and silk.

The great thing about collecting antique and early twentieth century shoes is that they are so evocative of an era, especially those dating from the Jazz Age of the 1920s and Hollywood's glamorous 1930s heyday, when women really did ooze elegance. Their dainty footwear mirrored their femininity and by purchasing heels from these decades you will be stepping back in time to when sophistication was the order of the day for style conscious women.

Pre-war shoes have their problems as leather dries out and satin shoes can become thin. So rather than wearing heels from the 1920s or 1930s it might be better to just collect and admire them. You can always treat yourself to a modern pair if you want to replicate the style.

Invest in a button hook if buying a pair of Victorian boots to wear as the small buttons can be tricky to fasten with your fingers.

A pair of Marie Antoinette's heels were sold at auction in 2012; in amazing condition, they were size 3.5 and made £6,000.

Genuine retro footwear

If you have decided that trying to hunt out these harder to find early heels is complicated then a great place to begin your collection is with the 1940s. There are many examples out there to buy at really affordable prices. These shoes also possess style but due to wartime shortages do not carry the rich embellishments of examples from earlier decades, so you are buying into a classic simplistic design that will always stand the test of time.

Moving into the 1950s and beyond is where shoe collecting can get really exciting because there is a wealth of styles and designs to choose from. Footwear turned a corner in the middle of the twentieth century and as a result, collectors recognise that it was an important period in fashion history. Sophisticated stiletto peep toe heels, 1960s knee high Go-go boots, vinyl sling-backs, 1970s platform soled boots and heavy *Holyrood* shoes have all become prized collector's items.

Plenty of sparkle and bling on Seventies boots from the glam rock period will make them more desirable, and the brighter the

Purchase antique shoes that are encrusted with rhinestones and possess big bold buckles or rich embellishments as the more lavish the decoration, the more desirable the shoes.

Many vintage shops, fairs and websites offer an array of shoes dating from the 1940s onwards, making these the perfect places to begin if you are considering starting a collection of vintage heels.

1940s ladies' sling back shoes with decorative pierce work.

disco shoes the better. Also, plastic PVC 1960s shoes will always attract a huge following. High end designer offerings such as those from Roger Vivier, Mary Quant or Vivienne Westwood will inevitably increase in value as demand is already high from collectors willing to pay hundreds of pounds in order to own original vintage designer footwear. In fact, when it comes to accumulating shoes from these decades, you normally need to be quick off the mark as great examples sell out fast and, more often than not, for high prices.

Condition is also paramount as collectors steer clear of shoes that have had the life worn out of them. So, before you buy, ensure that silk and satin shoes are not threadbare or covered in stains. Ensure all the beading and embellishments are still in place and that there is not too much wear to the sole or heel.

Mary Quant 1960s *Chelsea* boots with eyelet and buckle decoration.

As women used to have much smaller feet, many shoes dating right up to the 1980s are quite slender and often their sizing is not equivalent to today's. I wouldn't want you to purchase a stunning pair of shoes in your size because you believe they would be the perfect fit only to feel like an 'Ugly Sister' as you struggle to place the shoe on your foot. The golden rule is try before you buy if you intend to wear the shoes but if they are purely for display then shop away regardless of size.

Buy from reputable vintage fashion outlets, auction houses and dealers who can guarantee authenticity as there are (as with all shoes) vintage styles revisited on the market.

Contemporary Shoes

When it comes to modern shoe collecting it is true to say that the shoes you buy today could increase in value quite rapidly. I was approached by the weekly UK fashion magazine *Grazia* and asked if I would write a page on 'investment shoes'. I was thrilled and at once started to look at what I believed to be the perfect pairs from more recent decades, as well as some offerings from today's fashion industry that I thought would hit the spot for collectors now and in the future.

I decided to feature Chanel 'two-tone' pumps as they epitomize the brand and are a classic design; Yves Saint Laurent's *Tributes* which first debuted in 2006; Manolo Blahnik's heels; loafers by Tod Gommini and, of course, Vivienne Westwood's pirate boots which made their first catwalk appearance in 1981. Instantly recognizable as design classics, all these examples (and especially the older ones) are eagerly sourced by collectors and so should always retain their value.

Buyers beware of modern fake designer shoes as the market is overflowing with copies especially for up to date designs.

When thinking about contemporary shoes as collectables or for future investment, there are various factors to take into consideration. Think out of the box, and examine those heels that display an air of adventure; the more quirky they are, the more likely it is that they will become collectable. Limited edition shoes or those only available for a short period of time are definite must-haves, as are the aforementioned designer classics and those created out of collaborations as these all have the potential to increase in value.

In 2009 the highly regarded shoe designer Jimmy Choo collaborated with the retail chain H&M, offering an exclusive collection of shoes that could only be purchased from specific H&M stores. The collection sold out immediately and today they can only be bought on the internet for elevated prices. H&M also joined forces in 2012 with fashion journalist and *Vogue Japan* Editor-at-Large Anna Dello Russo. Within the glitzy collection were a range of extremely luxe heels but these stunning designs have not attained the same level of desirability as the H&M Jimmy Choo collaboration. This is probably due to Jimmy Choo being an internationally-renowned shoe designer whereas Russo is not a designer but someone recognized for wearing unique and innovative fashion. This is not to say that Russo's collection will never become desirable within collecting circles as time is also an important factor. Items which are not popular on release often become sought after decades later.

Manolo Blahnik feather heels.

Anna Dello Russo heels for H&M.

Artistic Heels

Shoes today are about much more than basic footwear functionality as they give their owners a chance to express their individuality and even their artistic sensibilities. Many who appreciate the aesthetics of shoe design collect and display them like precious artefacts in glass-fronted cabinets.

You only have to walk into the spectacular Shoe Galleries at London's Selfridges store for evidence that today we are blessed with exceptional talent when it comes to designing and producing jaw dropping heels. A sea of shoes beckons the consumer; there are enticing sculptural creations from the likes of Alexander McQueen, Nicholas Kirkwood and Rupert Sanderson as well as exquisitely embellished offerings from other commercially desirable designers including

Madonna is an avid shoe collector. She own hundreds of pairs, some of which she keeps wrapped in silk paper in her wardrobe. Although she never wears them, the iconic pop star occasionally takes them out to admire before carefully replacing them inside the wardrobe.

Giuseppe Zanotti and Christian Louboutin. All of these shoes have the potential to become future classics, just like those that we now eagerly seek from decades past.

Collect heels that you believe have the potential to become design classics of the future.

Innovation in shoe design may have reached new levels but the basic shoe shapes remain the same, so in reality these contemporary heels are all about the designer's personal vision. Some choose to concentrate on the shape or style of the footwear whilst others elaborately decorate a simple, classic shoe with rich materials or colour. Inspiration is drawn from a variety of mediums; traditional or historic influences are in abundance as is dramatising a shoe by implementing the designer's own visions and experiences. Naturalistic elements also rank high in shoe makers' concepts with Maï Lamore's opulent *Rose* shoes and McQueen's Monarch butterfly-thronged wedge sandals exquisitely showcasing this use of the natural world. Over the decades the heel has also become one of the most significant areas of the shoe for demonstrating elaborate design skills. From stiletto to wedge and platform to even triangular, the heel brandished with remarkable imagery has become a focal point on modern shoes.

In my opinion this is what shoes are all about. When I go shopping for a new pair of heels I steer clear of the mundane one-coloured sensible shoe and head straight for those that scream quirky and kooky individualism. I want the shoes I wear to get noticed so the more bizarre the better. All right, so I am a little extrovert anyway and these artistic designs suit my persona but I also feel that when you purchase artistic shoes you are buying a piece of art that has been lovingly created as a showpiece and, as such, should be treated with the respect it deserves by being exhibited on your feet. These are the shoes that I believe have collectable appeal, especially as many are already regarded as fashion collectables.

The majority of artistic shoes found in department and high street stores are still functional designs wearable by all those, like me, that adore cutting-edge fashions. However, there are also many shoes that have been created by talented avant-garde artists which could never adorn the feet in a practical sense. Taking the essential shoe shape as a blank canvas and then creating sculptural elements, these shoes draw the eyes of those that appreciate how well the fluid form of footwear lends itself to artistic styling. Even though they aren't necessarily wearable, these sculptural pieces merit attention as they can elevate shoes from simple fashion necessity to serious art form.

Take good care of your shoes. Modern designer pairs come with dust bags so where possible keep them inside these bags. Never place your shoes in direct sunlight as they can fade, and try to store in a cool, dry environment.

Maï Lamore *Rose* shoe heel with 18ct gold detailing.

Shoes designed as an art form

Transforming pairs of shoes to resemble teapots, banana skins and even shopping trolleys, a new breed of shoe designer has broken out from the conventional mould to deliver the most bizarre yet visually captivating footwear. All have the unique selling point of being one-offs as they are adapted for the wearer and all are bizarre, off the wall sculptures which entertain and delight those who come into contact with them. Funky footwear has become all the rage so it is no wonder that these extreme 'dare to be different' creations have become the fashion must-haves of late, as well as possessing all the hallmarks of heels that will eventually end up in museums if not snapped up by savvy, sharp-eyed collectors.

For me, collecting isn't just about amassing objects or acquiring rarity but about owning a piece of history that has somehow impacted on someone's life at some point. It is about appreciation, of the object as well as its past, buying into the idea that we are keeping something important alive by cherishing its existence. With fashion collectables, and in this case shoes, collectors are recognising their significance not only as wonderful footwear but also their back story, the social history behind their inception. I always say that every shoe can tell a story whether it is conjuring up memories of times past, tapping into an individual's personal nostalgia or simply representing the life and talents of the acclaimed designer who created it. So next time you purchase those heels feel comfortable in the knowledge that you are buying a piece of history that will touch your soul for ever more.

Buy into unusual design. Look for quirky, kooky and innovative shoes that instantly identify the designer that created them.

'*I actually have more shoes than anyone will ever know*'.

Tamara Mellon

Banana Split shoes by designer Kobi Levi.

Chapter 2

The History of Shoes

Footwear has always been a crucial part of our lives. We cannot leave the house without something on our feet, both to protect us from the elements and from the dangers of walking around barefoot. However, the design of footwear has progressed extensively over the centuries, from the leaves, bark and grasses used by ancient civilisations to the much more sturdy, glamorous and stylish designs we wear today.

Early Shoes

In *Collectable Names and Designs in Women's Fashion* I explained how Ötzi, a mummified Tyrolean iceman living in the Copper Age was discovered in 1991 wearing his original clothing with a shoe still attached to his foot. Made from a leather sole held together with a leather thong, this shoe also had a woven net of grass inside which was for holding hay in place to protect Ötzi from the cold weather. Using treated animal skins for the making of shoes was commonplace in colder climates and many fragments of early footwear have been discovered in excavation sites all around the world. However, finding Ötzi still wearing his whole shoe has been one of the most groundbreaking discoveries since it allowed experts to extensively examine footwear of the period. According to those experts, the construction of Ötzi's shoe was so complex that they believe even as far back as the Copper Age, people were working as cobblers or, in other words, earning their living by making shoes.

The oldest shoe in the world was a sandal made 8,000 years ago. It was discovered inside a cave in Missouri in the USA.

Egyptian flip-flops

Ötzi lived in a cold climate so his footwear was suitable for harsh weathers but for those residing in hotter parts of the world, the sandal was the favoured footwear.

They were created from woven palms, plant fibres and grasses which were attached to the foot with toe loops, and usually the end of the sandal was turned up. These early examples of shoes which are very reminiscent of today's flip-flops were worn by the

Egyptian flip-flop made of vegetable fibre.

Ancient Egyptians. On a recent trip to the Cairo museum I was surprised to see that on the inside of the sarcophagus walls there were paintings of these shoes. I soon learnt that although the majority of Egyptians spent their lives barefoot, those with a little money to spare bought sandals created from reeds and straw which they would wear on special occasions. The wealthy folk, meanwhile, wore sandals with leather soles and straps.

Ninety-three items of footwear were found amongst King Tutankhamen's treasures. Included were sandals made of wood which had depictions of his enemies on the sole, symbolising that with every step he took, the king would be treading on those that opposed him.

Roman Caliga

When examining ancient designs in shoes, it is those dating from the Roman era that start to give us the greatest insight into the many varied styles that were available as, fortunately, plenty of examples have been discovered and still exist.

Perhaps the most familiar style is the military *Caliga* which was worn by the Roman army when they arrived in Britain. These hobnailed shoes had open lattice work which exposed the toes and were laced at the front. A style that has been re-worked over the centuries, the more modern 'gladiator sandal' is a direct descendent of the *Caliga* and is

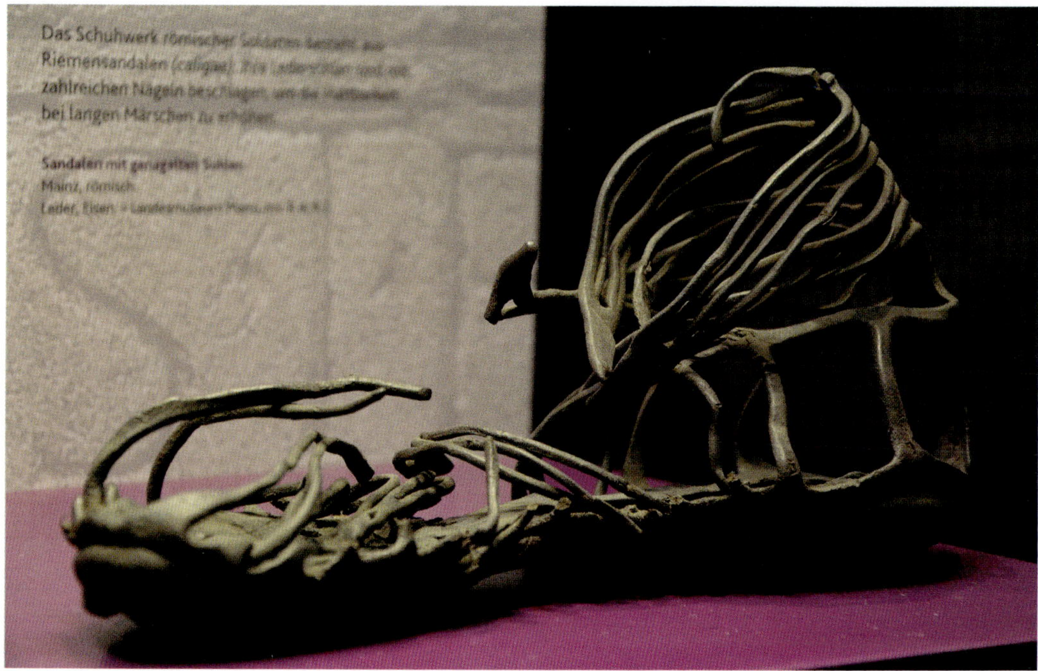

The Roman military *Caliga* shoe was hobnailed and had open lattice work which exposed the toes.

Poulaines, or *pikes* as they were also known, had extended toes as an indication of social standing whilst Tudor shoes developed into blunt toes.

very much at the height of fashion today when worn as a summer sandal.

Other styles popular throughout the Roman Empire were the *gallica* and the *calceus*, both of which were more appropriate for the British weather as they had closed toes.

The Roman Emperor Aurelian stated that only he and his successors were allowed to wear red sandals.

Medieval and Tudor Shoes

Known as *Poulaines*, *Crackowes* or *Pikes*, some shoes from the medieval era had ludicrously extended toes which indicated social standing; the longer the toes, the more important the wearer. In fact the shoes became so elongated, sometimes reaching to twenty-four inches in length, that walking often proved difficult. The way around this problem was to support the toe point with baleen, otherwise known as whalebone, or string that was tied to just below knee. Those in power actually tried to control the length of the shoes by passing laws that defined how long the *Poulaines* could be according to a person's class. The nobility, for example, were allowed longer shoes than peasants. However, these laws were never properly enforced and as a result they failed.

When the Tudor dynasty arrived in 1485, shoes began to take on a totally different look. Gone were the elongated *Poulaines* to be replaced by blunt, pointed toes which by the late 1500s had become more rounded in toe shape. Footwear up

Shoes have been discovered in buildings where they have been hidden to protect the house and the inhabitants from evil and misfortune.

to this period had always been flat but from the 1570s thick heels were being worn. By the end of the reign of Queen Elizabeth I in 1603, heels had grown to the height of three inches.

Seventeenth and eighteenth century shoes

Once the seventeenth century had arrived, women would wear shoes with pointed toes again, as they felt these to be more feminine. The buckle also played a large part of shoe design in this era for both men and women's footwear. Replacing ribbons, the buckle was used to fasten the shoes.

Moving into the eighteenth century, women started to become more concerned with the design of their shoes and showed a distinct preference for much more elaborate detailing. As a result, colourful embroidery, trimmings and metallic braid adorned

Shoes dating from 1725; the latchets [straps that fastened across the instep] were originally fastened with buckles.

footwear from this era. While the thick heels had slimmed down, unfortunately they were not that practical as the top of the heel was wider, thus losing strength to the thinner part at the base of the heel. This led to the heel gradually becoming lower before disappearing altogether for a short period at the end of the century. The shape of the shoe also changed, with an oval toe shape giving way to square. Also towards the last years of the century, there was a fashion for shoes created from delicate silks and satin with ribbons to fasten them instead of buckles.

Pre-Victorian shoes are eagerly collected by enthusiasts of period costume; however, they are becoming increasingly difficult to find, especially in good condition, so when discovered they can command a premium.

Nineteenth century shoes

This is the period which tends to attract the majority of antique shoe collectors, probably because footwear started to come into its own with regards to design progression. From lace-up boots to the simple pump, and with the high heel making a comeback along with big decorative buckles, the nineteenth century offered an abundance of diversity in footwear.

It was the boot that first became popular and continued as the most prolific form of footwear throughout the nineteenth century. Worn by both men and women, the *Blucher* boot is amongst the most well-known with its open front tab and lacing. There was also the elastic boot, the button boot and cloth boots. However, the most renowned design of the time displayed a closed tab with front lacing and was worn by Queen Victorian when visiting her Balmoral home in Scotland. This style has famously come to be known as the *Balmoral* ever since.

The court shoe style was another design that proliferated from the middle of the nineteenth century. First making an appearance in the 1860s, these flat shoes were produced in a variety of

A pair of French white satin flat pump shoes dating to the early part of the nineteenth century; these shoes have the wording *Droit* and *Gauche* inside each shoe, indicating right and left, along with the owner's name.

materials from silk and satin to leather and skin. More delicate and reminiscent, in my opinion, of a dainty ballet shoe, they were popular with women who would buy several pairs of exactly the same shoe as they could be worn on either foot. The result was that when one shoe had worn out, there was a replacement readily available.

Heels were back in vogue by the middle of the nineteenth century, gradually growing in size until they had become so ridiculously high that it was almost impossible to walk in them. The *Barrette* is a style which typically featured a ludicrously high heel, its name deriving from the bars and buttons that fastened the shoe.

A visit to the Northampton Shoe Museum is worthwhile as it houses over 12,000 pairs of shoes dating from 1620 to the present day. One of the many highlights in the collection is a pair of shoes worn by Queen Victoria on her wedding day in 1840. Made of white satin and trimmed with bands of ribbon, they were created by Gundry & Son, the shoemakers to the Queen, and are the epitome of Victorian style.

The nineteenth century also saw shoes start to feature ever more elaborate embellishments. Often they were embroidered with floral decoration on the toes, and ribbons were used to create single or multiple bows. Colourful metal threads were also used to adorn shoes.

As far as footwear was concerned, the twentieth century began much as the previous century had ended. Victorian boots remained fashionable daytime wear but evening shoes started to appear in a diverse array of styles. The Edwardian woman adopted a narrow shoe as this was seen as a sign of good breeding and gentility, usually in the style of a court with a small *Louis* heel which had already appeared in the Victorian era. Often, as in the previous century, these shoes would be adorned on the toe area with black jet beading, embroidery or metallic threads, as this was the only part of the shoe that could be seen under the long, floor-brushing skirt hemlines.

With the outbreak of the First World War in 1914, fashion of necessity took a back seat. Once the tumultuous conflict was finally over, however, it was time for a burst of confidence, colour and countless new fashion crazes as the frivolous, vibrant 1920s got underway.

Chapter 3

The Age of Jazz

> '*The wealthiest woman in the world couldn't pay me to make her an ugly pair of shoes*'.
>
> Andre Perugia

This is one of my favourite periods of the twentieth century as it really sparked the start of a brand new era. People made a conscious effort to put the hardships of the war years behind them as they looked forward to a promised future that would be brighter for all, while the female population prepared to face a world of new opportunities.

Having had to leave the home environment in order to tackle traditionally male-oriented jobs while their men were away at the Front, many women had

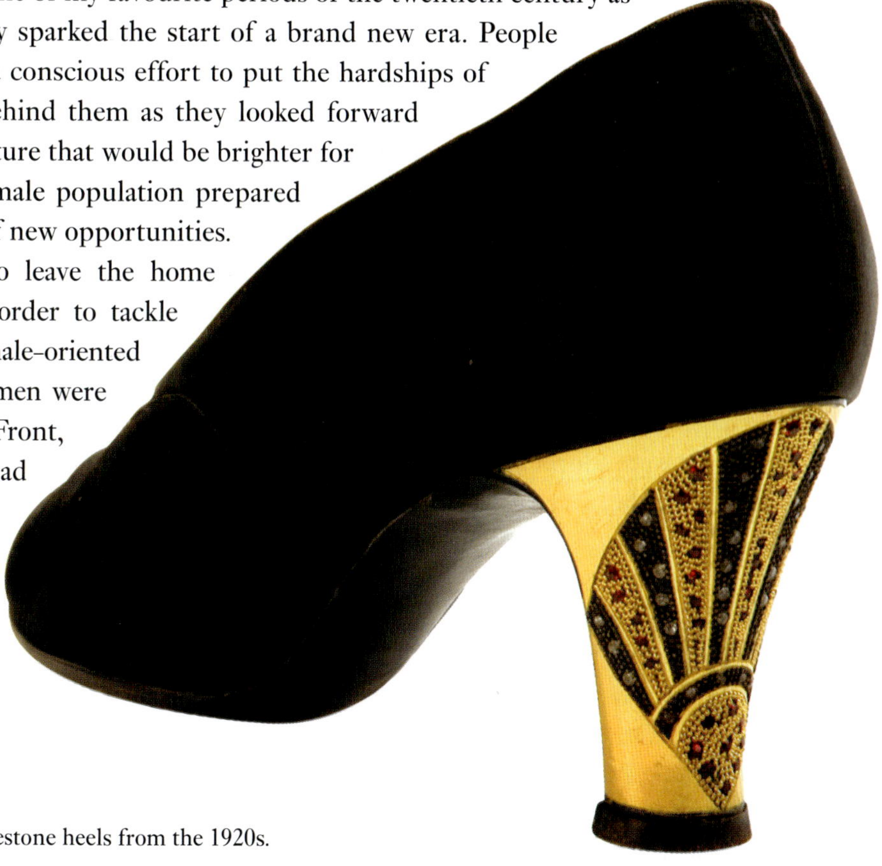

Decorated gold rhinestone heels from the 1920s.

discovered a taste for their new found freedom and were reluctant to go back to the old ways now the war had ended. Women aged thirty or over with property of their own were granted the right to vote in 1918, with all women over the age of twenty-one gaining the vote in 1928. Embracing their independence, the female population adjusted their attitudes to life, reflecting those adjustments in the clothes and accessories they chose to wear.

Out went the long skirts from the previous decade and in came much shorter, above-the-knee styles. The frivolous style was at its height with glamorous stars like Josephine Baker, Clara Bow and Olivia Thomas all flaunting the new flapper image of short bobbed hair and even shorter hemlines. Those same short hemlines meant that shoes were much more visible than before so now they, too, had to look fashionable and exciting. More than just a necessary finishing touch, the shoes worn by the dedicated flapper became the ultimate fashion statement, much like footwear is today.

> *'There is a certain tendency – to depart from the colours that would simply match clothes and to place a tone intentionally contrasting'.*
>
> *Vogue, 1921*

Shoe Styles

The 1920s 'Age of Jazz' footwear was loud, vibrant and colourful, just like the era in which it originated. The ankle strap button *Mary Jane* was a popular style as were T-bar shoes. They were stunning to look at and, crucially, comfortable to dance the Charleston in, and the most exciting examples of these shoes were extremely opulent. Produced in vivid fabrics, many were adorned with embroidery and encrusted with fake jewels and sequins, especially in the heel area which tended to carry crystal or beaded embellishments. This fancy footwear was the perfect embodiment of a decade that oozed confidence, jollity and a fresh new outlook on life for women.

The T-Strap

This style was perfect for holding the shoe in place while still showing off enough of the foot to entice. Originally the straps were thicker with no decoration but as time went on they became thinner and encrusted with sequins or rhinestones. Colours began as neutral black, brown and white but evolved into more vibrant shades, the satins and silks dyed to provide that splash of colour synonymous with the Jazz Age.

A pair of 1920s pearlized celluloid beaded heels in light blue, green and red half-beads on a celluloid pearlized white base; these rare items are worth over £1,000.

Mary Jane

A closed, low cut shoe with a single front strap was another popular shoe design in the 1920s. Leather was the norm for day wear while fabric Mary Janes would be worn into the evening, especially for more formal occasions. Some had eyelets through which fancy ribbon was threaded, and there was much focus on the heel area which would be covered with embellishments.

The name Mary Jane derives from a character of the same name in the *Buster Brown* comic strip that appeared in the *New York Herald* in 1902. They became a firm favourite with children of both sexes who clamoured to own them, and later on their popularity spread to women.

Oxfords

These sturdy, comfortable and almost utilitarian shoes were practical rather than pretty. Worn as everyday footwear they remained popular right through to the 1930s. Most were plain leather with cap toe and thick military style heel but there were two-tone

1920s shoe advertisement.

Deco tan and brown kid T-strap shoes with bronze jewel ornament.

colour options which became much more elaborate in the following decade. White canvas Oxfords were popular in summer months.

Strappy
Double, triple and criss-cross straps were also features of 20s footwear, either alone or with ankle straps.

Pumps
Inspired by eighteenth century court shoes and today a design classic, the pump shoe was also worn during the 1920s although it was less favoured than the Mary Jane or the T-strap. Many featured oversized tongues and big buckles and were made from luxe materials such as satin and velvet. Some featured two tone colour whilst others remained plain and simplistic.

Saddle Shoe
Sporty shoes, originally worn by men but adopted by ladies during this decade, remained popular until the middle of the century. With a two-tone colour scheme, usually white with a black saddle shape across the vamp, they had laces and low heels and were generally worn when participating in sports activities.

I. Miller vivid red velvet and gold overlay decorated flapper heels.

Ladies' 1920s Mary Jane and pump shoes.

Andre Perugia

'A pair of shoes must be perfect as an equation and adjusted down to the last millimetre, like a piece of engine'.

Andre Perugia

While many shoe designers began their illustrious careers during the 1920s, the one that made the biggest impact on footwear during the decade and beyond was Andre Perugia. The first notable shoe designer of the twentieth century, Perugia's initial designs mirrored the 1920s styles, often featuring a T-strap, geometric shaping and worked leather, but he also experimented with fantastical ideas that wouldn't look out of place today.

Innovative design and pursuing beauty was Perugia's intention which he accomplished by exploring with different shapes, new heel designs and customizing his shoes with unusual materials. His passion was driven by wanting to create aesthetic designs that shouted originality.

Born in France of Italian parentage, Perugia, who came from a long line of Italian shoemakers, trained at his father's workshop, proving himself an incredible prodigy. In

Perugia velvet pumps decorated with gold kid overlay.

Andre Perugia 1920s strappy shoes with diamante embellishment on tongue and heel.

Perugia gold and red leather evening shoes with richly decorated vamp.

1909, at the age of just sixteen, he opened his first shop in Paris, selling handmade shoes. Later he moved to the rue du Faubourg Saint-Honoré where all the major fashion designers had their salons. Although his innate talent made an immediate impact on the society ladies who shopped in the Faubourg Saint-Honoré, it was to be his association with world famous couturier Paul Poiret that assured Perugia's lasting success.

Perugia was known to talk to his shoes, which earned him the reputation of being something of an eccentric as well as a design genius.

A list of famous movie and theatre actresses made up his clientele as they all wanted shoes that represented the glamorous circles they moved in. The showbiz world was ideal for

The Padova brand was launched by Perugia in 1933. Exclusive rights to the brand in the US market were owned by Sax Fifth Avenue.

Perugia as it was full of fantasy and creativity, thus allowing his originality to shine out. In 1928, for example, he memorably transformed Josephine Baker's trademark turban into a quilted kidskin sandal while the 1929 *Mask* sandal is theatrical in every sense.

Throughout his career Perugia continued to push the boundaries of shoe design to the very limit. He enjoyed a long association with I. Miller & Sons who designed and made shoes for performers, movie stars and the general public, and during the 1960s he also worked for several years as a consultant with Charles Jourdan. Some of Perugia's ideas seemed plausible on paper but did not work that well in reality; one such design was the changeable heel shoe. The concept here was that a heel could be changed by sliding it along a track and then

Perugia worked as an engineer in an aircraft factory during the First World War.

securing it from under the sole, thus allowing the wearer to take their shoes from day to night or even for one pair of shoes to accessorize more than one outfit. Priced at $50 for a pair of pumps with a choice of two interchangeable heels, there was also an option to buy additional heels. Although it was a unique idea, women weren't ready for interchangeable heels and so this innovative idea failed to catch on.

Perugia's imaginative creations were often commissioned by fashion designers. Dating from 1938, his suede and monkey fur shoe

On his death in 1977 Perugia left his personal archive to shoe designer Charles Jourdan.

for Elsa Schiaparelli neatly demonstrate his originality. Perugia also merged his interest in art with shoe design. In 1931 his famous *fish* pump with decorative scales was a tribute

Andre Perugia's *Heel-Less* shoe, 1937.

to Georges Braque, the French Cubist artist, while the 1953 *Picasso* sandal paid homage to the great Pablo Picasso.

Probably the most recognized of all Perugia's innovative designs is the *Heel-Less* shoe created in 1937. This coral-coloured shoe with a curved wooden platform was considered extremely cutting edge as no-one had ever designed anything quite like it before. Today the gravity defying *Heel-Less* shoe is widely available in many different forms, proving indisputably that Andre Perugia was a design genius way ahead of his time.

Collecting tips

Perugia shoes are hard to come by and when they do appear on the market there is fierce competition between collectors to own them. I suggest starting with 1920s heels that are evocative of the era but do not necessarily have a designer price tag attached. Look for plain leather Mary Janes or T-bars which can be purchased for under £100. The more opulent the heels, the higher the price is likely to be but you can still pick up some fantastic examples, especially if prepared to buy from overseas.

Another tip with any form of collecting is the knowledge you acquire as the collection builds. The actual fun part, especially with the first half of the twentieth century, is doing the research, finding out where the shoe's life began. If a retailer's name is printed inside the shoe then you have the basic information to start to build up the shoe's story. Look at old magazine and newspaper adverts, research online to find out about the retailer including which designers, if any, they used. You might end up being pleasantly surprised as even though your shoes may not bear a designer name, they could turn out to be real treasures.

Chapter 4

The Glamorous Thirties

he world economy spiralled into a Great Depression in 1929 after the American stock market crashed. Gone were the vibrant times of the 1920s, only to be replaced by a dark cloud which hung continuously over this new decade. High unemployment meant that frivolous spending was out of the question and towards the end of the decade the threat of a new world war hung in the air. In order to avoid the harshness of everyday life, people turned to the silver screen as a form of escapism. Dressed in their glamorous outfits, the Hollywood screen stars projected a brighter, happier outlook on life. Eager to capture some of this glamour, ordinary people were soon imitating the style of idols such as Greta Gabo, Jean Harlow, Marlene Dietrich and Joan Crawford in their own wardrobes.

1930s white and leather shoes with Cuban heels and perforated decoration.

There was an extensive variety of shoe styles throughout the 1930s which followed over from the previous decade as well as coming back into fashion from past centuries. Oxfords, two strap shoes (high on the instep), round toed pumps, slip-ons and lace ups were amongst the styles worn, and all possessed some form of heel which gradually became lower during the decade. Black was the prominent colour for daywear although some women did opt for navy or maroon. Two-tone shoes were also at the height of fashion but they were very plain with no embellishment. Kid leather was the most prolific material used although crepe-de-chine and satin were popular choices for evening, usually in richer tones but sometimes in pastel hues. With the emphasis on glamour, reptile skin became a desirable option, representing luxury and status.

The strappy sandal which had not made an appearance since the Roman era made a belated comeback. Exposing the toes, it was the height of femininity and, combined with a high heel, was ideal for wearing with mid-length gowns to evening engagements.

A trademark of 1930s ladies' shoes is the small perforations used for decorative purposes. Similarly, cut-out designs were also popular, either open to expose some skin or with a contrasting colour underneath. Although most people wore closed toe shoes, you can find 1930s heels with a slight peep toe which just suggest a touch of feminine glamour.

This was a time for innovation, with the platform heel becoming popular from the mid-1930s. The most notable shoe invention of this decade was the wedge heel, created by Italian shoe designer, Salvatore Ferragamo.

Green satin with brocade shoes, 1930s.

Salvatore Ferragamo

*'There is no limit to beauty,
no saturation point in design,
no end to the material ...'*

Salvatore Ferragamo

'Shoemaker to the stars', Italian-born Salvatore Ferragamo is another celebrated twentieth century shoe designer whose incredible creations have influenced women's footwear for decades.

Born in the vicinity of Naples, Ferragamo showed an interest in shoe making from the age of nine when he made his first pair of shoes for his sister to wear at her confirmation. Two years later, Ferragamo began an apprenticeship with a shoe maker and then opened a small shoe shop from his parents' home where, together with six assistants, he created hand-stitched shoes for women. In 1914 he decided to emigrate from Italy to the USA in order to join one of his brothers who was working in Boston at a factory making cowboy boots. However, it was when Ferragamo convinced his brother to move with him to Santa Barbara and then to Hollywood that he really set off on the path to becoming one of the most renowned and iconic shoe designers of the twentieth century.

Ferragamo black satin three-layer wedge decorated with gold leather appliqué on the open toe vamp.

Having opened a small repair and made-to-measure shop, Ferragamo saw his designs become prized items amongst the Hollywood glitterati who wore his shoes both on and off the silver screen. Working with unorthodox materials became one of his trademarks; he is said to have used anything from candy wrapping and tree bark to hummingbird feathers and even a shawl.

Ferragamo once wrote that the 'women who come to me can be divided into the Cinderella, the Aristocrat, and the Venus ... Venus is usually a great beauty, of glamour and sophistication, yet under a glittering exterior she is often a homebody, loving simple things.'

There was, however, an issue with comfort as it seemed his shoes only satisfied the eye and not the feet. Knowing he had to rectify this problem, Ferragamo began to study chemical engineering, mathematics and human body anatomy at the University of Southern California. Having learnt that the weight of a body falls onto the arch of the foot, he was able to take his newfound knowledge and create a solution.

Having lived in the USA for thirteen years, Ferragamo returned to his native Italy in 1927, settling in Florence. With his shoes still very much in demand from high profile

Gold kidskin sandal with pyramid heel, 1930.

customers such as Marilyn Monroe and Eva Perón, Ferragamo set up his own workshop and concentrated on experimenting and perfecting his designs.

Although Ferragamo was an all-round design genius, he is more renowned for his spectacular innovative heels. Some say Howard Carter's discovery of the Egyptian King Tutankhamun's tomb in 1922 inspired the shoe designer to create sculptural shoes with heels that resemble inverted pyramids, although

Ferragamo invented a steel arch support which was inserted into the instep of his shoes, ensuring his stylish footwear was also comfortable.

A pair of Judy Garland's 'ruby slippers', created by Salvatore Ferragamo for the *Wizard of Oz* movie, made $666,000 at Christie's in 2000.

Judy Garland's 1938 *Rainbow* sandal.

it should be noted that he also took inspiration from Aztec pyramid shapes.

Ferragamo's cage heel was another design innovation, a brass construction wider at the top and tapering down to create an elegant high heel. But it was the cork wedge for which Ferragamo is most famous. The wedge was incorporated into many of his shoe designs with the best-known example being one worn by the actress Judy Garland in 1938. This *Rainbow* sandal was a tribute to her signature song, displaying a layered cork sole and heel covered in multi-coloured suede with gold strapping to the front and matching ankle strap. Other memorable Ferragamo designs include a patchwork wedge, Oriental toe and fluted layered cork wedge.

Throughout his lifetime Ferragamo was devoted to his work, inventing and patenting designs right up until his death in 1960. His creativity saw no bounds, his passion for design was relentless and the sheer volume of his brilliance is evident in the legacy he has left the fashion world. A true Italian craftsman, he understood that shoes were not just a necessity but true works of art.

Owned today by the Ferragamo family, the company continues to create stunning shoes along with a variety of other luxury goods.

Ferragamo designed at least forty pairs of shoes for Marilyn Monroe which she wore on many of her famous movies. For instance, she was wearing a pair of Salvatore Ferragamo shoes in the film *The Seven Year Itch* in the famous scene in which warm air from the subway grate lifts her skirt. Monroe was renowned for regularly wearing Ferragamo shoes. In 1999 the Salvatore Ferragamo Museum purchased at a Christie's auction a pair of red stiletto heels worn by the actress; with a price tag of $42,000, the shoes cost 1000 times more than their original retail price. In 2016, a pair of Monroe's white stilettos dating from the 1950s made $28,125 at Julien's Live Auctions in the US.

Collecting tips

Along with shoes from the previous decade, look for those that are evocative of the era, do your research and learn about the shoes. A great place to buy is on the internet from US dealers or auction sites because back in the 1930s many of the European shoe makers and designers sold their shoes through America's retail stores. The only issue is you will not have the opportunity to handle them and see their condition for yourself.

A museum dedicated to Ferragamo's life and work is open to the public in Palazzo Spini Feronoi, Florence. The late thirteenth century palace was bought by Ferragamo in 1938.

Suede patchwork wedge heel shoe.

Visit museums before you buy in order to get a feel for how genuine vintage shoes look. The V&A in London is ideal as it has shoes on permanent display. Many of the fashion museums such as The Bowes Museum in Co Durham and the Bath Costume Museum have shoe exhibits. Alternatively, look at your local museums to see if they have a costume section. Then, of courses, a visit to the Northampton Shoe Museum is recommended for any serious collector.

Vintage Ferragamo two-tone shoes.

Chapter 5

The War Years

With the outbreak of the Second World War in 1939, the 1940s began in a dark place. Women had returned to their roles within the working environment, filling in while the men were away fighting. Many joined the Land Army while others worked in munitions factories where the favoured footwear was hardwearing, practical and comfortable military styles. Austerity restrictions on the use of materials such as leather and rubber saw shoe makers adopt unusual alternatives such as raffia, cork and even cellophane, much like the revolutionary designs that Ferragamo had created in the

The 1940s.

previous decade. Women would 'make do or mend' with the clothes and shoes they already owned. In this austerity era, extravagance and wastefulness were impossible so everything was expected to last as long as possible.

In the resourceful spirit of the age, women would dye the shoes they already owned a different colour to match an outfit.

The rationing of clothes, cloth and footwear was introduced in June 1941 in order to ensure the fair distribution of these items. Utility clothing was later introduced as it had become apparent that even with rationing in place, controls needed to be enforced on quality and price. The government ruled that it was illegal and unpatriotic to embellish clothes for sale, and that manufacturers creating utility wear under the CC41 (clothing control 1941) label were forbidden to use unnecessary buttons, elaborate trimmings or extra stitching for any items of clothing, including shoes. As a direct consequence of these austerity measures, considerations of style and artistry during this period were largely abandoned in favour of conservative, practical footwear that was fit for purpose.

1940s slingback heeled shoes with diamond cut out and stud detail.

Even though Britain and Europe had been hit hard by the war, across the Atlantic in the United States restrictions were initially less stringent. While British women were rationed to just two pairs of shoes a year, their American cousins were allowed three pairs annually up until March 1944 when leather shortages reduced the ration to two pairs.

In wartime Britain, women would swap their sensible daytime shoes for more elegant heels during the evening; however, these would be shoes that they had owned before the outbreak of war.

Red Cross Shoes

The origins of America's biggest shoe manufacturer date back to the 1870s in Cincinnati, Ohio. At a time when there was no difference between left and right shoes and all were the same width, there was a competitive yet concentrated shoe making industry. Factories employed German immigrants to learn the skills of shoe making, and their descendants later went on to open their own shoe making businesses. Two of these descendants, Irwin Krohn and Samuel Fechheimer, founded Krohn-Feccheimer in 1896. Krohn was aware that a brand name would create an identity which customers could recognise, and it would also work well for advertising purposes. So, in the mid-1890s Red Cross Shoes was born. Together with savvy advertising of the 'noiseless' shoe, the brand was a huge success.

However, with the onset of the First World War, the high top shoes they had been making went out of fashion and this, coupled with the six-month shoe makers' strike of 1921, created difficulties within the industry. In an attempt to rectify matters, Lewis S. Rosenthal, a local industrialist, initiated an idea to merge eight shoe factories and form the United States Shoe Company. This, however, did not solve the problem as a lack of marketing resulted in poor sales. It was Joseph S. Stern who brought them back from the brink. Stern's shoe company, Stern-Auer, agreed to merge with the United States Shoe Company on the condition they could be in charge of marketing. Recognizing the previous success of the Red Cross Shoes, he set about his marketing plan by offering them at a cheaper price. By 1939 Red Cross Shoes were so popular that demand exceeded production, leading to phenomenal success for the United States Shoe Company.

In 1941 the company designed the official Women's Army Corp shoes. However, the American Red Cross was not happy with the Red Cross name being linked to a commercial concern since Red Cross Shoes had nothing to do with the humanitarian organisation. In consequence, the Foreign Affairs committee proposed banning the name but to avoid this, the shoe company agreed to suspend use of the Red Cross Shoes brand name for the duration of the war. In 1948 the Federal Trade Commission permitted the reinstating of the Red Cross Shoes name on condition that a public disclaimer was issued, asserting that the brand had no association with the American Red Cross.

By the mid-1950s shoe production had reached 100,000 pairs a week with the United States Shoe Company leading the way in the manufacture of ladies' footwear. The company

Red Cross Shoe fashion advertisement, 1943.

Red Cross Shoe advertisement, 1945.

did diversify into other areas over the following decades, becoming involved in ladies' apparel and specialist eyewear. Today the company is owned by the Luxottica Group which owns many eyewear retail companies while the United States Shoe Company continues as a subsidiary.

The CC mark was designed by Reginald Shipp, a commercial designer, and stood for 'Controlled Commodity'.

Collecting 1940s shoes

Fashion in general from the 1940s has appeal with vintage seekers as this was a transitional period between the more austere 1930s and the affluent 1950s. It was also a time that gave women a renewed freedom outside the domestic sphere. Filling in at the workplace while the men were away fighting, women wore fashions that represented their strength and versatility.

Rationing in Britain was on a points system. Adults were originally allowed sixty-six points for clothing every year but in 1942 this was decreased to forty-eight points and was further reduced to just twenty-four points in 1945. A new pair of shoes used seven points so careful consideration was obviously required when contemplating a purchase; could the old ones

It can be difficult to tell the difference between true vintage 1940s ladies' shoes and more modern styles as many of these designs have been revisited over the decades. The 1980s, for instance, saw a trend for 1940s fashion and so the style was replicated, meaning there are loads of shoes around that look as though they date from the 1940s but actually date from the 1980s.

be made to last any longer or was a new pair absolutely essential? These questions required cautious consideration in order to ensure that the precious points were used wisely.

In America rationing on leather footwear began on 7 February 1943 allowing men, women and children to buy up to three pairs of leather shoes a year with designated ration stamps. However, in 1944 the allowance was dropped to only two pairs a year.

Even though strict rationing was in place during the war years there are great examples of genuine 1940s shoes available for the collector, especially from the USA because they were in greater supply there during the austerity years.

When seeking British 1940s footwear look for original ration shoes that carry the CC41 utility logo inside. This was the British Board of Trade requirement on all clothing and footwear.

Ration shoes tend to be very basic and were made to be worn constantly so as I always stress, check condition. Some of the utility shoes do appear on the market with little intricacies added but this is rare.

You either have to trust your instinct and buy heels that you are sure are genuinely period or else buy from a trusted vintage fashion shop/auction that has the expertise to accurately date their fashion items.

Chapter 6

The Fabulous Fifties

*I*t was the post-war years which saw a dramatic turn in the progression of shoe design with many innovative new styles, designs and designers all coming to the forefront. Experimental footwear such as the *Heel-Less* court shoe first created by Andre Perugia (see Chapter 3) gave the illusion that the wearer was suspended in the air. Pinet was soon to follow with the same design concept but unfortunately these shoes failed to win popularity.

With the austerity years of the 1940s receding to a distant memory and the economy on the road to recovery, there were many successful designs that changed the face of fashion in a positive way with one of the most important new fashion collections, launched by Christian Dior in 1947, setting the tone for the next decade. The *New Look* was a complete contrast to the harsh fashions of earlier years; this collection brought back the feminine silhouette with tight fitting bodice, vast skirts with petticoats underneath, wasp waist lines and softer, delicate shoulders. Dior's collection initiated a brighter future for fashion which demanded shoe designs that complemented the overall silhouette.

One of the most dramatic, ground-breaking designs revived during this decade was the stiletto heel. Documented as being around as early as the 1800s, this slender heel or the 'little dagger' as it came to be known, has been attributed to iconic French shoe designer Roger Vivier who brought it back into fashion while he was working for Dior in the 1950s. Vivier's innovative, modern interpretation of the stiletto was much thinner than its previous incarnation as he used a steel rod to manufacture an ultra-thin heel which in 1954 increased from 6 to 8cm in height and was termed the *Aiguille Stiletto*.

The word stiletto derives from *Stylus* which means a pin or stalk. This term refers to the metal pin that runs through the length of the heel to reinforce it.

Shoe advertisement, 1950s.

Roger Vivier

'To be carried by shoes, winged by them. To wear dreams on one's feet is to begin to give reality to one's dreams'.

Roger Vivier

Often referred to as the Fabergé of footwear, Roger Vivier was a sculptural genius when it came to heel design as, aside from the stiletto, he also created the *Comma*, *Pyramid* and *Escargot* heels to name just a few. Working alongside some of the biggest

Roger Vivier produced a pair of gold kidskin heels studded with garnets for Queen Elizabeth to wear to her coronation in 1953.

names in fashion, Vivier created shoes that complemented and completed their high trend ensembles and so it didn't take long for him to become one of the most sought after shoe designers of the decade.

His avant-garde designs have always been at the cutting edge of fashion although they are also deemed design classics. Elsa Schiaparelli was the first fashion designer to

Vivier's black *Belle* pumps with oversize diamante buckle.

recognise Vivier's gift for shoe design by including his shocking platform shoe in her 1938 collection and his ten-year association with couturier Christian Dior is testament to Vivier's talent.

Vivier believed his designs to be more than fashion; to him, they were sculptures with rich and extravagant decoration. Constantly experimenting, Vivier pushed the boundaries of shoe design. In the 1940s he was the first designer to create shoes made of clear plastic which progressed into a full range during the 1960s. His unusual *Croc Heel* appeared in 1959; it was slender, with a slight curve outwards which gave an air of elegance that was both sophisticated and chic.

Opening his own fashion house on rue François-ler in Paris in 1963, Vivier continued to work for other fashion designers such as Yves Saint Laurent and Balmain. At the same time he concentrated on experimenting with his heel designs, releasing the curved

Modern Vivier Stiletto Rose Heels.

Vergule heel in the same year, followed by his more recognized shoe design, the *Belle* pump, which is sometimes referred to as a pilgrim pump. Worlds apart from his stiletto, this shoe with a low square heel and oversized metal square buckle on the front became a signature piece of Vivier's collections. Still produced today by the company in a variety of different materials, colours and heel types, the *Belle* pump with its clean, simple lines is a timeless shoe classic that has become just one of the beautiful shoe legacies that Vivier has left behind.

> *'High heels are a paradox, they can make a woman appear more – or less – powerful'.*
>
> Vogue

1950s Shoe Styles

It wasn't only the heel that became the focus of shoe design during this decade as the toe also came into the spotlight. The *winklepickers* were the chosen footwear for British rock and roll fans of both sexes. With their long and sharp pointed toes, the shoes reminded people of the pin used to extract a winkle from its shell, and thus they acquired the *winklepicker* name.

In fact there was quite a mix of different shoes styles in the 1950s, including the *Opera* pump, the wedge, strappy sandals and ballet pumps. Exposing the toes was deemed feminine with an array of peep toe shoes on offer. Slingback shoes were also worn as throughout the 1950s the heel of the foot was considered erotic, and thin strapped evening sandals were also a sexy evening alternative. Flatties looked great as daywear with Capri-pants, a firm favourite with

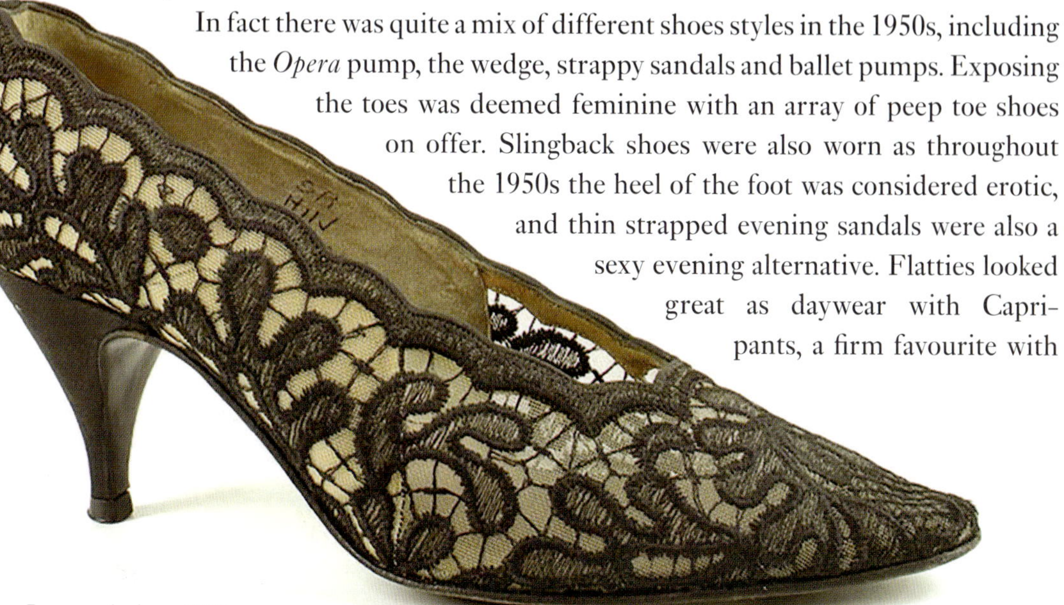

Lacework shoe, 1950s.

A pair of Gina court shoes with orange flame toes.

the actress Audrey Hepburn. Wedges, a style made popular in the previous decade, were again perfect for adding lift to the heel area in the 1950s and, believe it or not, the thronged flip flop came into fashion with women and younger girls, although the noise they made caused them to be less popular with men.

The importance of 1950s shoes lay in complementing the outfit and wearing footwear that matched ladies' other accessories such as handbags, belts and gloves.

Gina Shoes was established in 1954 in London by Mehmet Kurdash. He named the company after his muse, the movie star Gina Lollobrigida. Only using the best materials, the shoemaker put his emphasis on quality with everything created by hand. Still made in London, today the family-run company is a highly regarded and recognised brand in the luxury shoes and handbag market.

In 1909 Coco Chanel opened her first shop in Paris and ever since then the Chanel label has produced ground-breaking fashion statements. From the 'little black dress' to tweed suits, Chanel has an aptitude for producing stylish signature pieces. Two-tone pumps are classic Chanel and as a result are considered iconic. Again, these shoes epitomise Chanel and as a result are considered 'must-haves' for collectors. Invest in the new season's examples and you will always have a pair of shoes that will mature with age both in style and price.

The ubiquitous *Oxford Saddle* shoes were ideal for wearing with the fashionably vast skirts when out dancing while loafers and a variety of winter boots were also worn for casual activities. Yet it was the stiletto and the kitten heel that personified stylish elegance of this decade. The trend was for understatement with simple designs in single colours, although Coco Chanel bucked the trend towards the end of the decade with her legendary two–tone slingback pumps in beige with a black toe, which were introduced in 1957.

Collecting 1950s footwear

The 1950s is a fun era in which to begin a vintage shoe collection. With so many styles on offer there is something to satisfy all preferences. You can choose between the stylish stiletto and the more robust dancing pumps, or else concentrate on just acquiring shoes

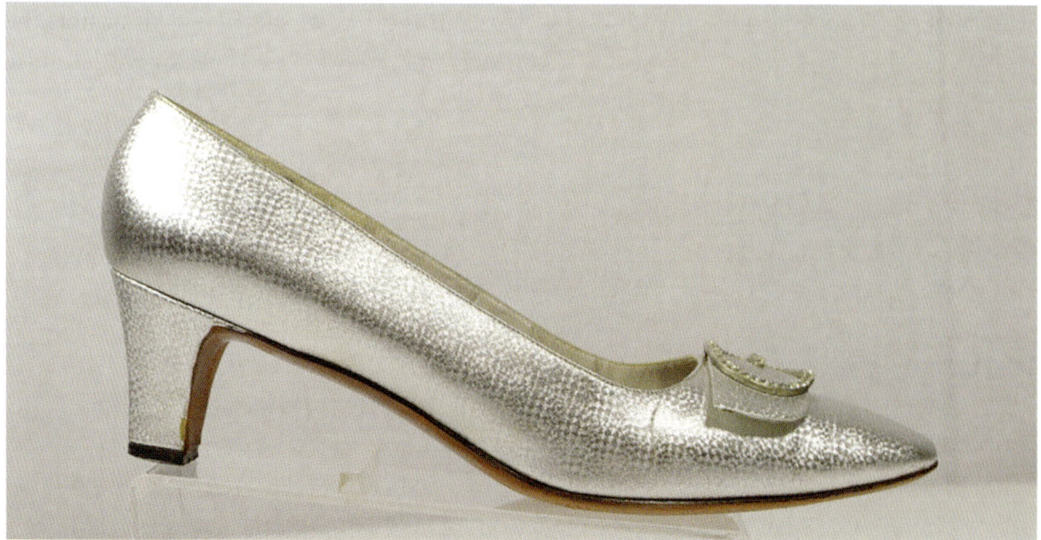

Roger Vivier silver pump heels.

that display an unusual embellished heel. Some collectors prefer to base their shoe collections around footwear from a specific maker or designer.

Roger Vivier began working for Delman Shoes before moving on to the more elite end of the market. Those seeking a pair of Vivier heels on a budget are advised to seek out examples from this early part of his career. Another idea is to buy shoes created for retailers like Harrods in London and Saks Fifth Avenue in New York as many prestigious shoemakers produced lines for the retail market.

Unusual designs always stand the test of time so source 1950s shoes that have statement heel decoration. Although many pairs were plain, there was also much emphasis placed on the heel area during this decade so it is possible to find ladies' shoes with carved Lucite heels, heavily embellished with jewels or just with the heel taking a unique shape.

As with any fashion collecting you are buying into a moment of history so try to buy the best you can afford that is representative of that era.

A pair of Andrew Geller heel shoes bought from Harvey Nichols by 'queen of style' Wallis Simpson in the 1950s recently sold for £950 at auction.

In 2011 a special pair of evening shoes made for Princess Soraya of Iran sold at auction for a staggering $26,629. These kitten heel shoes crafted with topaz and silver threads had been designed by Roger Vivier for the princess back in 1962; now it was the turn of the design house to buy them back as part of its commitment to recovering some of its greatest works. These heels are believed to be the most expensive shoes to be sold at auction anywhere in the world.

Chapter 7

The Swinging Sixties

Britain had recovered, the economy was thriving and a brand new fashion scene had emerged. Once again people had freedom of choice, throwing themselves into the exciting new fashions, cultural interests and social scenes that dominated the decade. A new, free-spirited 'Youthquake' generation was born out of the post-war baby boomers and they were looking to break free from the constraints of their elders which they achieved predominantly through fashion and music.

Mass produced, throwaway fashion reigned supreme. Cheaper than couture, it allowed women to own dozens of pairs of shoes, most of which were purchased from retail outlets and the new fashion boutiques that became a 1960s phenomenon. Vibrant hues were on offer from the vast palette of colours and psychedelic swirls in bright pink, greens and turquoises were also available to those who had a more adventurous fashion taste, as were blocks of colour, op-art black and white along with space age styles later into the decade.

The development of new synthetic materials meant that vinyl and shiny patent plastic shoes were all the rage, available in a variety of colours and usually sporting a small kitten heel.

Styles such as the pointed-toe stiletto and round-toe heel pump crossed over from the previous decade and the single strap Mary Jane was widely worn, but with the funky new street style fashions replacing high end couture, other shoe styles became more prevalent. The boot was favoured, especially when worn with the new *Mod* style mini-skirt; referred to as the Go-go boot it could be between calf and knee length with a low or flat heel and displaying either a chiselled, round or pointed toe.

The elastic-sided *Chelsea* boot was another popular form of footwear which made a reappearance during the 1960s. Having been fashionable some 125 years previously, it became a popstar favourite with *The Beatles* being mainly responsible for its resurrection as a footwear sensation. A direct descendent of the Victorian boot, the *Beatle Boots*, as they came to be called, were tight fitting and ankle length with Cuban heels and a sharp, pointed toe. Inspired by the craze, British fashion designer Mary Quant produced her own plastic version for women which came in a range of colours.

Mondrian was an iconic design which was originally introduced in the form of a dress by Yves Saint Laurent in 1965. Inspired by a painting by Piet Mondrian, this design began to appear on a variety of fashion items throughout the 1960s.

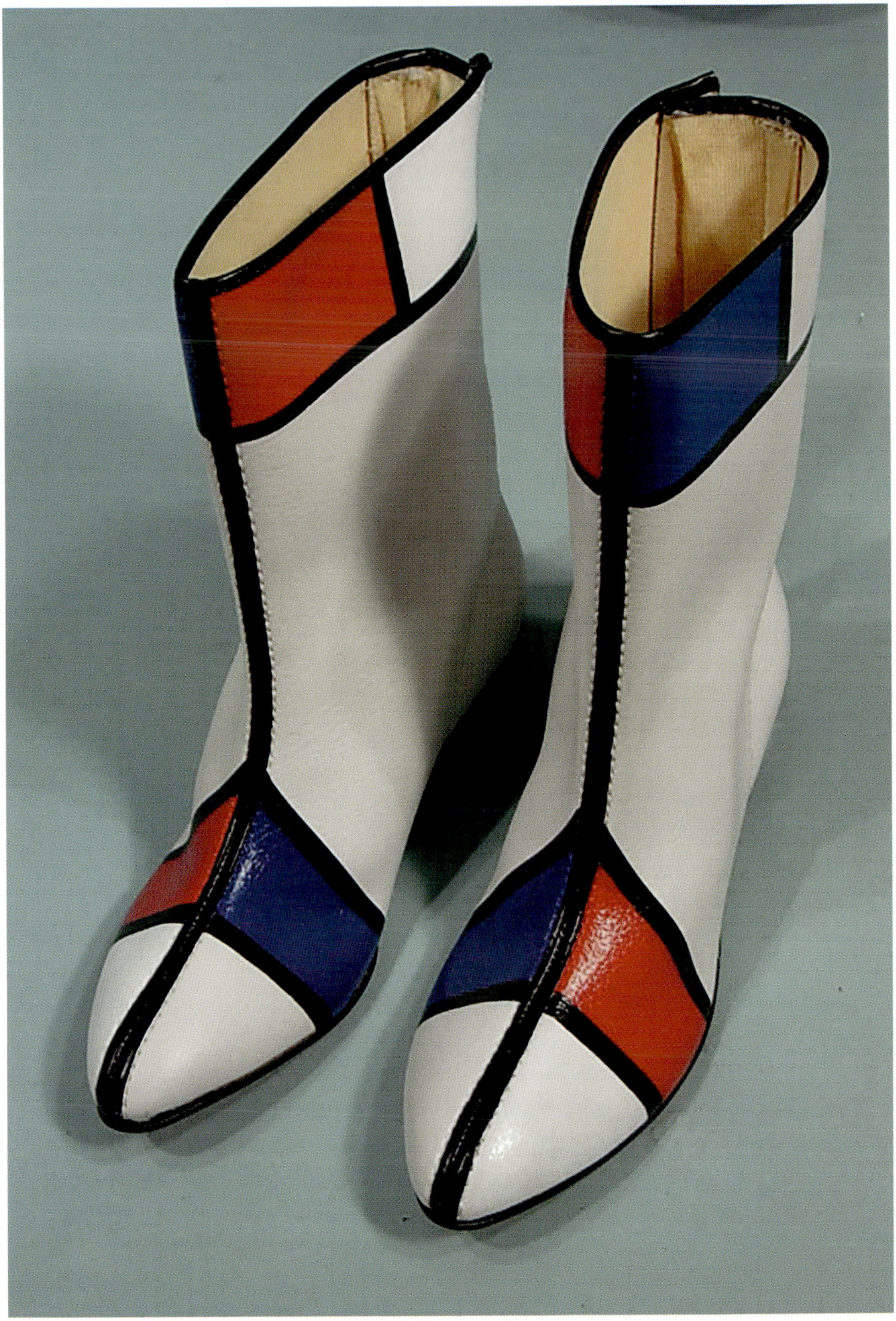

A very rare pair of 1960s Op–Art Mondrian designed Go-go boots.

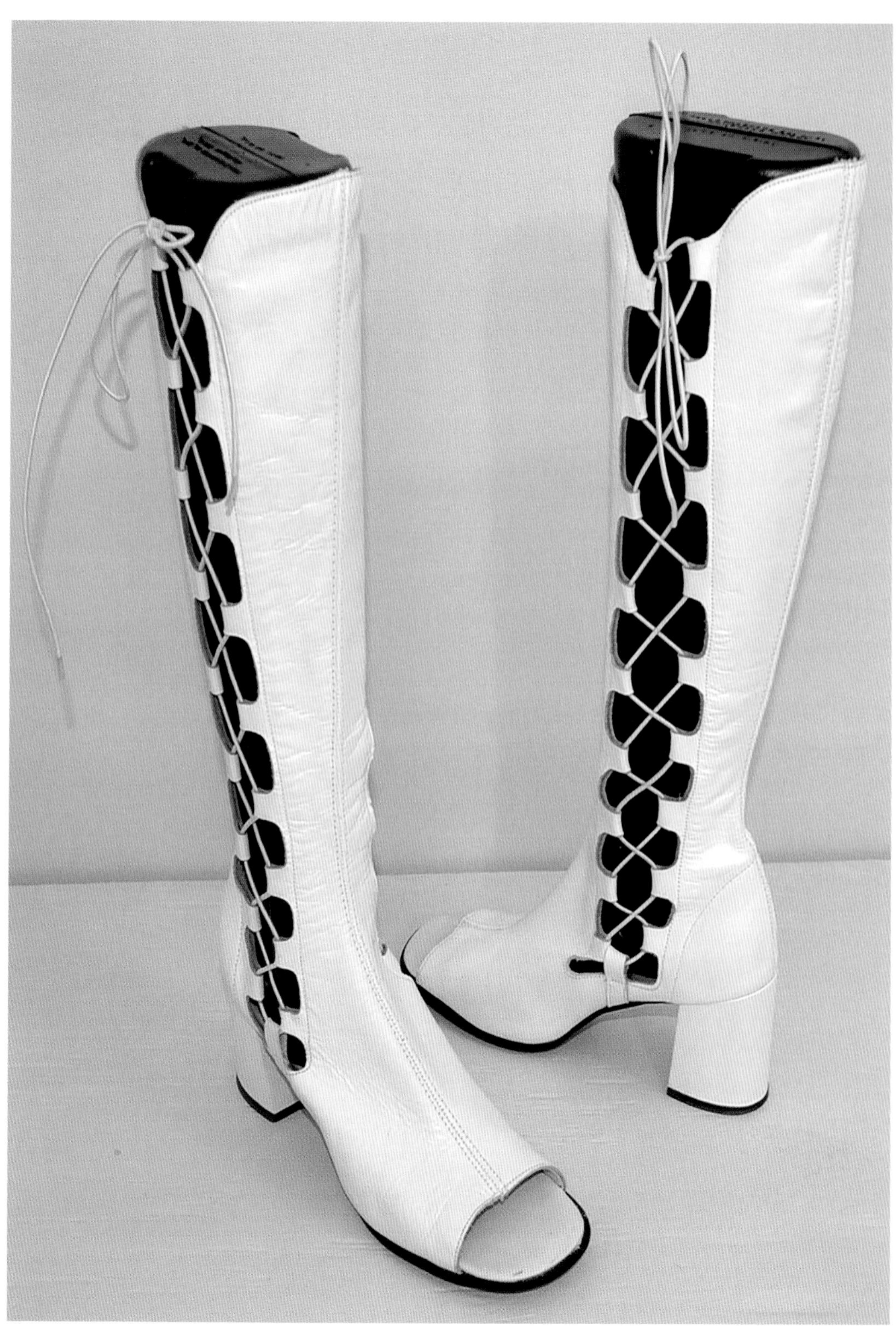

Knee-high 1960s Go-go boots with cut out design, block heel and peep toe.

Mary Quant

> ‘Snobbery has gone out of fashion, and in our shops you will find duchesses jostling with typists to buy the same dresses’.
>
> *Mary Quant*

One of the most memorable names in fashion when it comes to the 1960s is Mary Quant. Her minimalist *Mod* fashions were desired by everyone. Her artistic background began when Quant attended Goldsmiths College in London where she gained a diploma in Art Education and went on to become an apprentice milliner. Setting up her boutique *Bazaar* in 1955, she wanted to sell relaxed clothes that were, she said, ‘suited to the actions of life’ and embarked on a journey of designing and making her own range of dresses that soon became sell out successes. In 1963 she opened her second shop in London's fashionable Knightsbridge district, and became the first winner of the ‘Dress of the Year’ award.

Quant also sold shoes under the ‘Afoot’ label which she launched in 1967. Known as the *Quant-Afoot* boots, they had detachable tops. They could be worn as long boots but when unzipped the top could be detached, just leaving boot shoes. You could also mix

Mary Quant plastic *Chelsea* boots with metal eyelet decoration.

Mary Quant bright yellow *Chelsea* boots, 1960s.

and match different coloured tops if you owned more than one pair. Created from clear plastic over a coloured lining, the heels were moulded with Quant's signature 'Daisy' motif so that when it rained the wearer would leave a trail of daisy footprints behind her after walking in a puddle. Today these boots are the amongst the most desirable of all 1960s footwear as they were ground-breaking designs at the time and now represent an era that basically launched fashion as we know it today.

Space Age

High end fashion designers were still experimenting with their own designs, working with different materials and gaining inspiration from things that were happening in society at the time. One of the most notable trends was for 'Space Age' influenced clothing which graced all the catwalks. Space exploration boomed in the 1960s with the pinnacle being the historic moment when Neil Armstrong stepped onto the moon in 1969. British designer John Bates, along with Paco Rabanne, Pierrre Cardin and Andre Courreges, are the designers most renowned for injecting space travel influences into their lines.

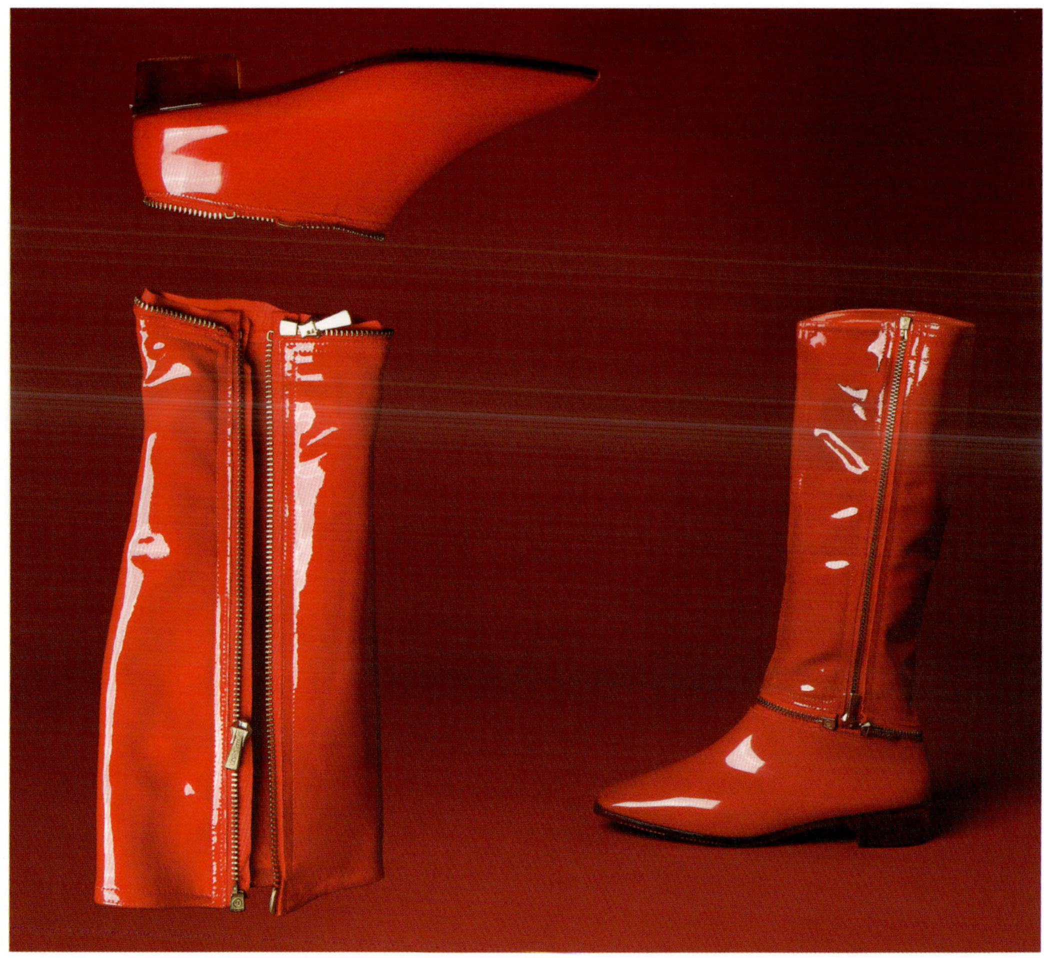

Mary Quant scarlet *Quant-Afoot* plastic zipper boots.

With shiny materials like vinyl, sequins, PVC and even glass in their designs, these out-of-this-world fashions included dresses, skirts and crazy headwear with visors, with silvery metallics, white, red and fluorescent shades as the dominating colours. The look was completed, of course, with long, tight Space Age boots in the same colour palettes.

Dr Martens

The 1960s also saw the inception of one of the most classic boot designs of the twentieth

Today Dr Martens are eagerly sourced by collectors with prices varying according to age, condition and style. Look out for limited edition pairs such as the *Hello Kitty Sanrio* which can make over £200, or those covered in floral decoration which can command between £150–£200.

Dr Marten *Castel* boots in yellow and black stripes.

century. The first ever pair of cherry red, eight-eyelet Dr Martens work boots rolled off the production line on 1 April 1960, a date that gave the boots the style number 1460. The *Mods* were the first to adopt this boot as their own but over the decades, members of various youth subcultures including Skins, Punks and Goths have made these boots with their air-cushioned soles part of their identity, as have followers of certain types of music such as Ska and Psychobilly.

Collecting 1960s shoes

Shoes from the 1960s make a loud and bold statement, adding vibrancy to any collection. The eclectic mix of designs, materials and colours makes this era one of the most satisfying. Look for shoes that scream 1960s in bright colour palettes, Op-Art imagery and a kaleidoscope of patterns, as these are the most desirable.

Kingfisher blue vinyl shoes with buckle decoration and slingback.

Well-known names in footwear command a premium. For example, Mary Quant boots can sell for upwards of £200 depending on condition, and examples from higher end designers sometimes cost thousands of pounds. Nevertheless, it is possible to find many genuine vintage pairs at more affordable prices because they don't have a designer name attached to them.

It is imperative, especially with 1960s plastic/vinyl shoes, to check condition. It is almost impossible to repair vinyl so if the zip has gone it cannot be replaced and any splits mean the shoes are a lost cause. Also steer clear of fading or severe scratches.

Psychedelic slip on loafers.

Chapter 8

The Disco Years

Confusion reigned during the 1970s as far as fashion was concerned with a plethora of contrasting styles vying for prominence. Glam rock, flower power, punk and disco fever were all in the spotlight at some time during the decade but there is one iconic fashion design that always springs to mind when thinking about the 1970s, and that is the sky-high platform.

Having made short appearances throughout history from as far back as the Ancient Greeks, the platform shoe shot to fame once again when re-popularised by the glam rock pop idols of the 1970s. This flamboyant musical movement of heavy make-up, copious amounts of glitter and adventurous costumes was led by the likes of David Bowie and T-Rex. An over-the-top, extrovert style, it was only truly complete when finished with a pair of platform sole shoes or boots.

The cult 1975 movie *Tommy* also influenced the platform fashion as the 'Pinball Wizard' played by Elton John wore 'cherry red' Dr Martens which were moulded in fibre glass and stood a staggering 4ft 6.5ins high. Over time these boots have become as iconic as the film and can be viewed at the Northampton Shoe Museum where they are on loan from the R Griggs Group Ltd, the makers of Dr Martens who purchased them at auction when Elton John sold them in 1988 through Sotheby's.

Terry De Havilland

'I consider myself the rock-n-roll cobbler. That's exactly what I am. I always was'.

Terry De Havilland

In my personal opinion there is only one shoemaker synonymous with the 1970s platform and that is British shoe designer, Terry De Havilland.

Terry De Havilland *Bowie* platform boots.

Terry De Havilland's 1973 dragon platform in green suede.

De Havilland possesses an innately theatrical spirit which is reflected in his designs, instantly attracting popstars, film stars and other celebrities who appreciate the designer's dramatic 1970s shoes.

De Havilland's original 1974 *Luna* shoe, created from metallic python skin in a pop art design, was a firm favourite with rock stars' girlfriends at the time due to the pioneering use of metallic python skin. The five-tier wedge was also popular for being world's apart from the 1960s winklepickers and pumps. In a nutshell, De Havilland's designs were new, fresh and exciting.

A-list names such as Britt Ekland, David Bowie, Debbie Harry, Bianca Jagger and Bette Midler have all stepped out in De Havilland's platform and wedge heels. These well-known stars were also responsible for inspiring De Havilland's *Zebedee* shoe which displayed an unusual 'spring' heel. In the 1970s he designed Tim Curry's shoes for the *Rocky Horror Show* and two decades later created Angelina Jolie's boots for the hit film *Tomb Raider*.

De Havilland was five when he first started helping out at Waverley Shoes, his parents' footwear company located in London's East End. Recalling these early days, he says:

> '*Shoes are in my psyche, as my first memory is of my mother's platform shoes with ankle straps which filled the house and were made by my father*'.

While on leave from National Service in 1957 De Havilland cut his first pair of shoes for the family business. In 1964 he designed his own first pair; worn by his model girlfriend, they were spotted by Annie Traherne, Editor of fashion magazine *Queen*. Traherne featured the shoes in the magazine and this exposure projected De Havilland's designs into the limelight, ultimately resulting in the opening of his first store, *Cobblers to the World*, in London's

The gold *Bowie* boot was made for a Bowie collaboration with famed photographer Mick Rock and features Mick's work.

Zebedee shoe in metallic python with 'spring' heel, 1979.

The *Margaux* wedge was born in 1973 and is now a classic De Havilland design.

fashionable King's Road in 1972. Soon his platforms and wedges had gained such huge popularity that everybody who was anybody owned a pair of Terry De Havilland shoes. By the 1980s, De Havilland was making over 800 pairs of shoes a day. Setting up under another label, *Kamikaze*, the shoemaker concentrated on creating shoes for the emerging punk and goth sub-cultures. However, this company was forced out of business in the late 1980s due to Dr Martens and the new trainers becoming the new fashion must-haves. De Havilland continued to work and it was the shoes he created for Anna Sui and Paco Rabanne's runways shows in 1997 that put him back under the spotlight.

Today Terry De Havilland shoes are a worldwide brand and remain very much in the same vein as his 1970s designs. Many, such as the *Geisha* wedges, are styles he originally created during his early career and provide the mainstay of his collections. The *Geisha* wedge is a bestseller favoured by today's A-listers even though it was designed over forty-five years ago. In 2013, the version featured a geisha illustration by artist Tiff McGuiness and was available in gold, navy, black and red. The *Luna* shoe is also still made today although it is cut a little wider on the foot than its predecessor.

Collecting De Havilland shoes

This iconic shoemaker's designs are the defining shape of a decade. They instantly scream 1970s with their vibrant colours, sky-high heels and outrageous designs, with the added advantage of having a great British designer name attached. You really cannot go wrong if you choose to invest in De Havilland shoes; vintage pairs are selling for high prices at auction and the modern examples that mirror the 1970s designs are also desirable with those that appreciate the eccentricity of years gone by.

In 2012 handbag designer Anya Hindmarch teamed up with De Havilland to create a range of shoes that tied in with her season's *All I've Ever Wanted* range inspired by the wrappings of Quality Street chocolates. The vintage-inspired platform shoe came in a choice of twelve colour ranges housed in amazing, innovative packaging. Resembling a vintage toy box with a transparent window in eye-catching lilac, it was entitled 'the all singing, all dancing shoe' by Anya. This brilliant collaboration has resulted in a must-own footwear collectable. Definitely one for the future although this boxed pair of shoes has already been snapped up by both the style savvy and those who recognize a good investment.

Vintage Terry De Havilland can be sourced from a wide variety of places including charity shops, car boot sales and auction houses. They are so evocative of their era that people recognise the 1970s style but not necessarily that they are designed by such a prestigious designer so they can slip through the net. More modern De Havilland can also be bought quite easily on the internet; prices are reasonable and if buying from the most up-to-date ranges it is often possible to find them offered on sale in online retail with discounts of as much as fifty per cent. You cannot go wrong investing in this great designer's offerings as they are shoes that not only look amazing but also play an integral part in shoe history.

Terry De Havilland *Geisha* wedge, 2013. with artistry by Tiff McGuiness.

Thea Cadabra

'Wearing wonderful shoes is a truly uplifting experience'.

Thea Cadabra

The 1970s was a time of eccentric innovation; budding new designers were able to showcase their talent to the world with no real barriers. Some chose to launch their ranges to a wider audience while others created shoes for their own personal satisfaction. Thea Cadabra (who kindly wrote the Forward to this book) was and still is a remarkable

Thea Cadabra *All Weather* shoe, 1978.

shoemaker who self-designed shoes as one-offs throughout the 1970s and 1980s as private commissions but really for her own pleasure. Experimenting with styles and materials, working with inspiration from all elements of life she is now classed as one of the most notable shoe designers of the twentieth century.

Thea Cadabra is a master in the art of design innovation. Her wild and wonderful creations in sculptural footwear are works of art that wouldn't look out of place in a gallery. Her ability is to showcase flights of fantasy combined with elements of humour that are injected with dramatic theatrical influences, ensuring that each pair of Cadabra's shoes express their own unique personality.

You only have to examine the 1978 *All Weather* shoe to see that Cadabra's passion for experimentation and love of bold colours sets her aside from more conventional shoe designers. Developed from her grey and silver *Storm* shoes, Cadabra enlarged the theme to encompass the sun, clouds, lightening, rain, rainbow and blue sky. The clouds are appliquéd with a prismatic plastic *Shimmertex*, giving a rainbow hue as is the rainbow itself. These shoes are on permanent display in the Northampton Shoe Museum in the United Kingdom.

Cadabra's career
Regarding her shoes as timeless classics that are not dependent on fashion trends, Cadabra is passionate about making beautiful distinctive shoes.

The *Suspender* shoe, 1977 and the *Vampire Bat* shoe, 1978.

She first ventured into shoe design back in the 1970s after graduating from university in 1973 with a degree in Russian and Turkish. After years of academic study, Cadabra now yearned for a more creative way of life and so, more by chance than a planned career move, she stumbled into designing shoes. She approached Turkish shoemaker Mehmet K. Egeli in London and explained, in Turkish, that she wanted to learn how to make shoes. Egeli felt this was a sign from Allah and thus Cadabra immediately began to learn her trade on a one-to-one basis from a master craftsman.

The *Suspender Shoe* was originally created by Cadabra to complement a leather mini skirt which had pink ribbon lacing the sides and worn with seamed stockings. Today this original design has been reissued and forms part of her *Boudoir Collection* which is handcrafted in a small artisanal factory in Italy.

Cadabra was soon designing her own brightly coloured thematic handmade shoes which she would wear to London parties in the 1970s.

The *Bat* shoes in blooded leather and rich black suede were originally designed by Cadabra to wear to a Halloween party. The bats have wired wings and the bodies are made from carved cork. Glittery rhinestones suggest stars in the night sky.

By 1975 she had set up her own workshop and was taking private commissions. In 1979 she received First Prize in the Crafts Council Shoe Show for her *Lunar Lopez* shoe. This design is made with a moulded leather outer shell over an inner form, and the space between is filled with kapok. The wedge encloses a rechargeable electric battery set

Lunar Lopez with rechargeable electric battery set in rubber in order to shock proof it.

in rubber to render it shock proof. Yellow lights flash along the *fuselage* while red lights rotate around the rocket-style base at the back of the shoe. This award was responsible for launching Cadabra's reputation as an innovative designer and became the springboard for her successful career.

The following year Cadabra moved to a larger house in the East End of London to accommodate her workshop. However, she wasn't to stay long as a high level of street violence forced her to move to a more tranquil way of life in the South of France.

This change of lifestyle wasn't to prove fruitful as moving away from the big city meant that Cadabra lost her client base. So, in the mid-1980s she abandoned hand making and began work as a designer at the Bureau de Style of the Charles Jourdan shoe factory in Rome. This was her entrée into the commercial world of design. She later worked freelance for US companies before finally moving across the Atlantic to work full time in the United States.

A stray bullet from a gun came through Thea's window and embedded itself in the ceiling of her Whitechapel home.

The *Dragon* shoe, 1978.

After more than twenty years within the commercial sector, Cadabra decided to return to the United Kingdom in 2004. She has now re-established her own studio and is concentrating on producing ever more stunning designs which are sure to create a frenzy among those who appreciate only the best when it comes to desirable and exotic shoes.

These theatrical *Dragon* shoes were made as a commission for a delightful customer called 'China.' They were Cadabra's interpretation using the theme of her name. Over a hundred pattern pieces have gone into the making of this colourful and dramatic shoe.

The *Ice Cream* shoe, 1981.

The red mane is wired and has foam padding for 2-D effect, and the eyes are made from leather-covered cork.

These innovative *Ice Cream* shoes were born of an idea that came to Cadabra when she was sitting on the top deck of a bus looking down on an ice cream van. She was musing about how the shapes of an ice cream and cone could lend themselves to a shoe, using the cones as a heel and the ice cream as a decorative vamp with its chocolate sauce, patent red cherry and vertical wired wafer.

Inspirational designs and freedom of spirit
Cadabra explores an array of diverse sources when looking for inspiration. Her original 1970s and 1980s shoes were influenced by social events of the time such as *The Rocky*

Thea Cadabra creates shoes from the heart and will only ever make shoes that she is happy to wear herself.

Lilac Water Lily shoe, 2010.

Horror Show, the stage production that became *The Rocky Horror Picture Show* in 1975. The fashion boutique *Biba* founded by Barbara Hulanicki has also inspired Cadabra's work, as have vintage clothes, 1950s kitsch and even David Bowie. Her newer designs celebrate the world of dance in a range of *Tango* shoes created from glittery leathers and her *Water Lily* creations embody the true Cadabra style with three dimensional motifs.

Water lilies were the theme of Cadabra's debut boutique range launched in 2010. Once again the use of vibrant multi-coloured textural combinations trademarks Cadabra's brilliant designs. The original 1983 pale turquoise sandal is also on permanent display at the Northampton Shoe Museum.

Possessing a freedom of spirit which is mirrored in her creations, Cadabra makes shoes that exude so much fun, vibrancy, delightfulness and uniqueness that only the most self-assured and confident women are able to wear them. This talented shoe designer prides herself on the fact that her footwear is made with great passion 'and loves and likes to think that those who buy them passionately love wearing them.'

Palm Tree shoe, 1983.

This elegant and exotic shoe, with its delicately carved heel by jeweller James Rooke, is a beautiful, labour-intensive work of art. The palm leaves are individually wired so the fronds can splay out, and facetted beads cluster at the base like dates. The yellow version of this *Palm Tree* shoe is in the shoe collection of the National Gallery in Victoria, Australia.

Collectable Cadabra

The black lace, kid leather *Maid* shoe is the epitome of elegant seductive sauciness. The sculptured heels by jeweller James Rooke are in the form of a pair of curvaceous female legs below a flounced white bow which provides the back of the maid's apron, forming the pretty vamp. This style has been reissued as part of Cadabra's *Boudoir Collection*, together with the *Suspender* shoe. As each pair is handmade, they are definitely worth acquiring for your shoe collection.

From a collecting perspective Cadabra's shoe designs tick all the right boxes. They are unique in style with a distinctive novelty factor that appeals to those thirsty for original design. The fact that each one is handcrafted means that no two pairs are identical, and Thea Cadabra has already gained great respect from the fashion and arts industry as her shoes are on permanent display in a number of museums around the world.

Maid shoe, 1981.

Thea's *Flower* shoes in red patent leather.

Although all of this amounts to shoes with undeniable investment potential, they should also be worn, admired and talked about. Cadabra footwear forms part of our social history and as a result it should be treated with the respect it deserves. So buy a pair, wear them, admire them and finally take good care of them because these shoes are your own exhibits for the future.

Buy Cadabra's shoes now as this talented designer's offerings are set to rocket in both desirability and price in years to come.

Manolo Blahnik and the stiletto

While the platform soles were the most ubiquitous design of the 1970s, they were not particularly practical or comfortable. Reportedly, A&E departments were full of people with sprained or broken ankles who had fallen over when wearing these ridiculously high heels. So, when Spanish shoe designer Manolo Blahnik turned his back on the chunky platform in the 1970s and instead concentrated on bringing attention to the stiletto heel, it was a refreshing and sensible alternative.

Coliflor (S/S11), a dazzling turquoise pump with two layers of rippled cut suede; the inspiration behind the design is from the gardens of Blahnik's house in the Canary Islands and the rounded cut-outs mimic cauliflower.

'I believe a confident, sensuous walk will make any woman, anywhere in the world, wear my shoes beautifully'.

Manolo Blahnik, Stylist Magazine

Most people think that it was Carrie Bradshaw, the character played by actress Sarah Jessica Parker in the hit television series *Sex and the City* who first propelled Manolo Blahnik's fabulous heels into the spotlight when she begged a mugger to take anything but her precious strappy Manolos. Yet the truth is that the name of this iconic shoe designer has long been familiar to women who adore sexy, fun and feminine footwear.

Since the early 1970s Spanish born Blahnik has been renowned for creating desirable and sumptuous mules, pumps, slippers and, of course, the mainstay of his shoe collections, those sexy stiletto heels. He has worked alongside some of the biggest names in fashion including Ossie Clark, John Galliano and Caroline Herrara. A self-taught shoe designer, he is responsible for some of the most innovative shoe creations to walk the fashion runways and holds the accolade of being the first man, in 1974, to adorn the cover of British *Vogue* magazine. Blahnik is also the first shoe designer to have his work celebrated at the London Design Museum. His creative and enchanting heels have for decades held women spellbound around the globe. Blahnik believes that 'shoes transform a woman' with each pair representing a 'fleeting moment' in time that has been captured. Legendary designs which create shoe envy among those that appreciate sensual, sophisticated and pure classical style, his creations have cemented Manolo Blahnik's place in the fashion history books as one of our most celebrated shoe designers.

Blahnik designed the gold sandals Bianca Jagger wore when she rode a white horse into *Studio 54* on her 30th birthday.

Blahnik's Spanish mother and Czech father hoped their son would become a diplomat. He enrolled at a university in Geneva to study politics but after only one term he switched his studies to architecture and literature. In 1965 he travelled to Paris to study art and afterwards his father sent him to London to perfect his English. There, Blahnik spent much of his time watching films in cinemas, earning money by working in boutiques and doing occasional design jobs. In 1970

Mirto Green (A/W10); this deep green Blahnik shoe has a distinctly 1970s feel to the design.

he travelled to New York with a portfolio of drawings, hoping to gain employment as a set designer. It was here that Blahnik met with Diane Vreeland, Editor of American *Vogue*, who instantly fell in love with his amusing drawings of accessories and suggested that he learnt how to make shoes.

Visiting factories, Blahnik began to learn the art of shoe making by talking to machine operators, pattern cutters and technicians. He then returned to London and set about designing men's shoes. However, the young designer found these a little too restrictive as he couldn't find ways of improving on the brogue design so made the decision to venture into the world of women's shoes instead. Not keen on the platform and chunky heels that were mainstream 1970s fashion at the time, Blahnik focused on the more elegant stiletto heel which immediately ensured that his designs stood out from the clumpy alternatives. It was when approached by the famous British fashion designer Ossie Clarke, who asked Blahnik to make shoes to complement his fashion lines at his runway shows, that Blahnik's reputation as a shoe designer blossomed. In 1973 he was able to open his first boutique in London's Chelsea.

A meticulous craftsman, Manolo Blahnik works alone and is solely responsible for every sketch and prototype pair of heels that bears his name. Masterfully sketching the design using a *Tombo* Japanese brush pen, he then carves the beechwood last before sculpting the heel, first by machine and then carved with a chisel and filed by hand. The aluminium mould is then made of the last before the final plastic version from which the shoe will be produced.

These expertly designed shoes are unique as they incorporate all the elements that femininity demands from a ladies' stiletto heel but in an adventurous and

Blahnik's *Cherry* shoe designed for Ossie Clarke's 1971 fashion show at the Royal Court Theatre has become iconic. This shoe was re-issued by Blahnik in 1996 after the tragic death of the fashion designer.

Blahnik Black and white *Nepala* print court shoe.

architectural style. Quoted in the *New York Times*, Blahnik says that 'you walk differently in high heels – and with a shoe that is uncomfortable you walk badly. So the shoe has to be light, beautifully centred, the heel balanced to perfection.'

It is this attention to detail that has given Blahnik the respect and credibility that he deserves from all the women around the world that adore his shoes. He has been nicknamed 'the godfather of sole' by supermodel Naomi Campbell, and his shoes have been described as 'better than sex' by Madonna. A true artisan who has mastered the art of creating shoes that evoke simple elegance, Blahnik is correct in saying 'my shoes are special shoes for discerning feet.'

> *'I never wear flats. My shoes are so high that sometimes when I step out of them, people look around in confusion and ask, "Where'd she go?" and I have to say, "I'm down here."*
>
> Marian Keyes, author

Collecting Blahniks

The biggest collector of Manolo Blahnik shoes is none other than Manolo Blahnik. The designer admits to owning over 25,000 prototype pairs which are split between his homes in London and Bath. In fact, he is quoted as saying he doesn't live in a house, he lives in a shoe museum. He did, however, lose 300 pairs in a flood in London but says, 'that's ok because I saved some of them.'

The rest of us can only dream about owning a handful of his exquisite heels so, when it comes to buying with a view to the shoes becoming desirable future fashion collectables, which ones should we all be looking for? The satin *Swan* pump, encrusted with crystal beaded vine appliqué angled across the vamp and outer side, which was famously worn by Bella Swan in the movie *Twilight Saga: Breaking Dawn Part 1*, is a definite consideration for your collection as this divine shoe has been captured in time on the silver screen. The same goes for the pairs adored by the character Carrie Bradshaw in *Sex and the City*, such as the *Something Blue* shoes featuring crystal brooch detail on the vamp, and the *Campari* Mary Jane heels.

In 1997 Blahnik created the shoes for John Galliano's first couture collection for Christian Dior.

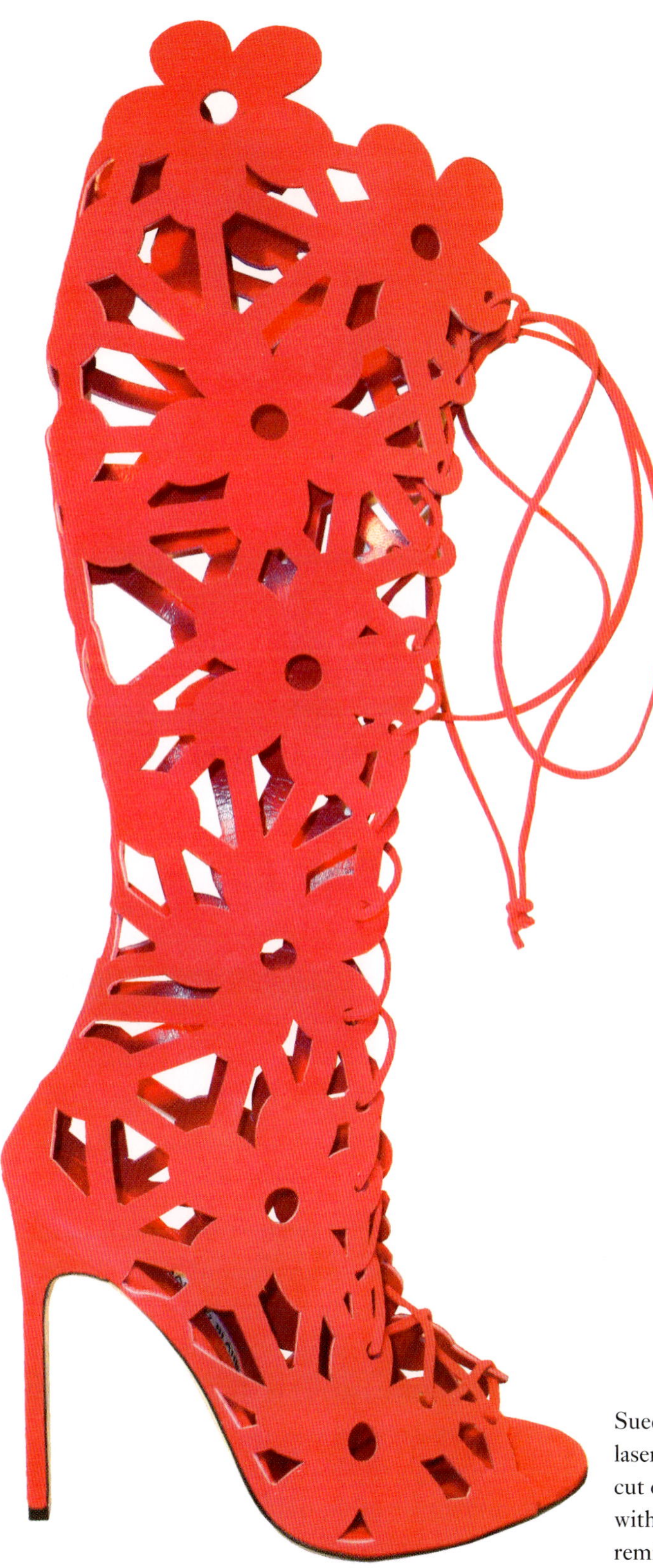

Suede shocking pink *Kahika* floral laser cut lace up boots; the all over cut out detail of flowers combined with the slender knee high design is reminiscent of Swinging Sixties styles.

Bella Swan pumps encrusted with crystal beading vine appliqué angled across the vamp and outer side.

Vintage and classic designs are also a must for collectors and have the advantage of being less expensive to buy than the current Blahnik heels. Many examples can be found on internet auction sites or specialist dress agencies that deal in second-hand designer fashion. Be warned, though, as with any sought after high end designer, there are now a plethora of fakes on the market, so only ever buy from a reputable retailer or dealer and where possible make sure the shoes have their original packaging, box and receipt as provenance. However, if you can get the actual designer to sign your shoes then you have all the provenance you need along with an iconic autograph and a pair of desirable shoes, although you will probably never be able to wear them in fear of the signature rubbing off.

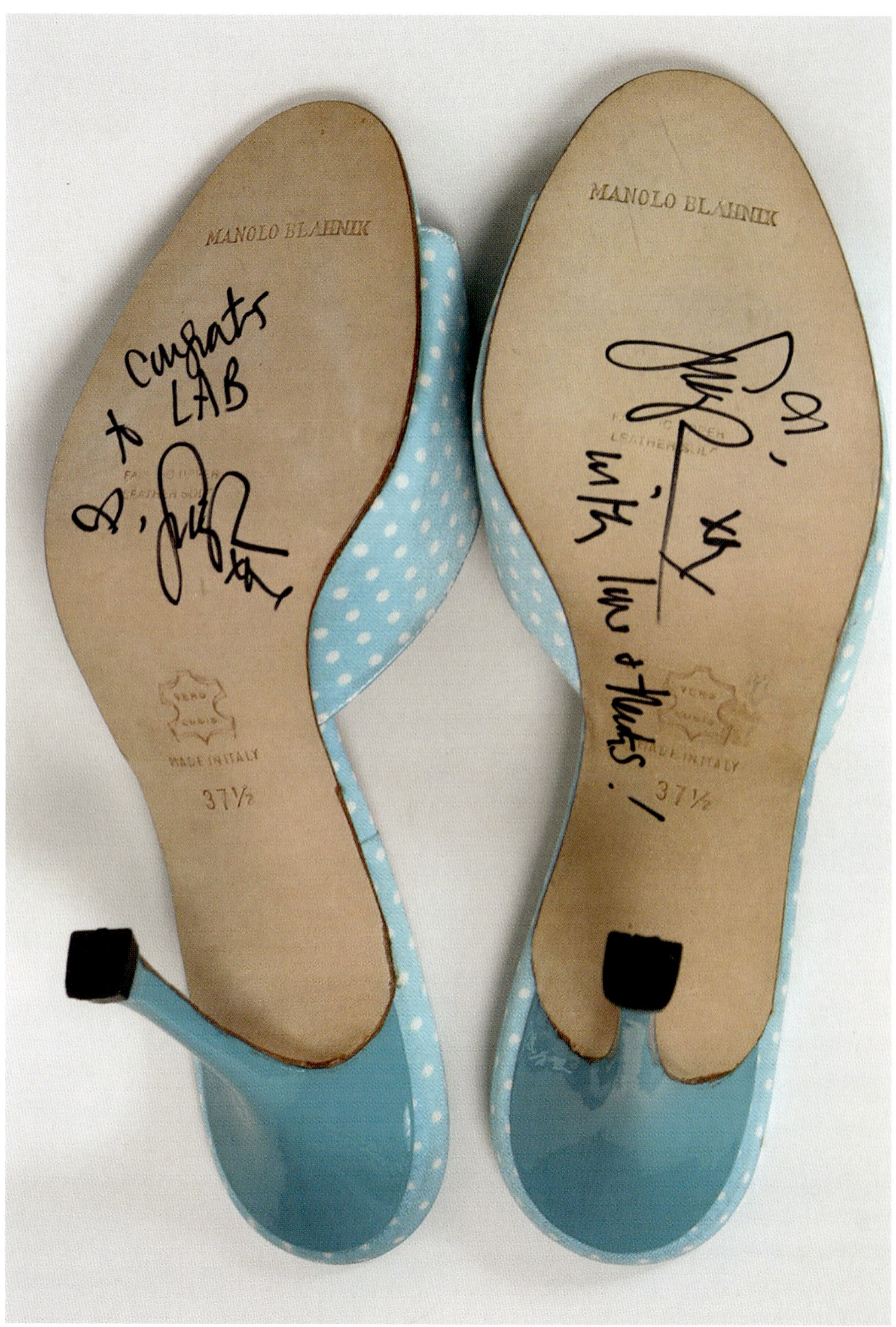

A pair of heels signed on the sole by Manolo Blahnik.

Sabratha Beige Tweed, a Liberty exclusive, featured cut out detail at the ankle and contoured shape; it tied with leather twine which could be replaced with ribbon by the wearer for a new look for the evening, and was available in both grey and beige tweed.

Another savvy collectable option is shoes that have been created in collaboration with a retail outlet as they can only be bought through that store. In September 2010 Blahnik did just this with *Liberty of London* and it was the first time ever that Blahnik's designs had been sold outside his flagship store in the UK. He produced an exclusive range of commissioned designs including limited edition heels created using 1960s Liberty fabric.

Sub-Cultures in the 1970s

As previously mentioned, Dr Martens became hugely popular in the 1970s and were the footwear of choice for skinheads and the new punk movement which emerged towards the later part of the decade.

The designer most associated with the punk movement is Vivienne Westwood (see Chapter 9) who, together with her partner Malcolm McLaren, exploded onto the fashion scene with their seditious punk clothing. The ranges consisted of anarchic t-shirts, bondage trousers and anti-establishment wear. Westwood is also renowned for creating

Gene, another Liberty exclusive, was produced in an iconic Liberty print and also featured a black buckle as detail on the vamp.

some of the most notable designs in shoes throughout her career. Early designs such as the 1973/74 *Goat Chain* boots, produced under the *Sex* label, and the *Seditionaries* boots of 1976 which first displayed Westwood's now trademark straps and buckles, set the stage for the commendable and ground-breaking footwear designs she continued to create throughout the ensuing decades.

Collecting the 1970s

A wealth of true vintage 1970s shoes are out there ready to be snapped up by eagle-eyed collectors. Non-designer knee-high platform boots can range in price from £200 to over £500 depending on the colour, style and condition. Platform shoes are slightly cheaper but be aware that the platform was revisited in the 1990s with styles almost identical to that of the earlier decade.

For a subtle classic 1970s style, find neutral black and brown heels that represent the decade in softer form as they are wearable, affordable and a great place to start collecting. The more hardened collector might want to source 'way out' shoes that are evocative of the era, featuring patterns of lightning strikes or with rainbow colours adorning the boots, since these decorations are desirable. Cut out designs, unusual patterns and, of course, the obligatory glitter always command a premium. The chunkier the sole and heel the better on platform shoes.

Vivienne Westwood *Goat Chain* boots, 1973.

Since its inception in the 1930s the loafer has become a classic casual wear design which has a massive following among collectors, and none more so than Tod's *Gommini* loafer. Originally created in the 1970s by Diego Della Valle, the founder's son, this classic example was hand sewn and had a distinctive modern design. Ever since it has become a signature

You can have so much fun collecting footwear from the 1970s as the shoes themselves are outrageous and flamboyant feats of craftsmanship that define their decade.

shoe and as a result the *Gommini* stands tall in the shoe collecting market. Again, vintage 1970s examples are snapped up by keen-eyed collectors and although they don't command huge amounts of money, generally costing around the £200–£300 mark, these loafers are still very much part of 1970s fashion history.

Classic style 1970s black platform heels with knot design on the vamp.

Chapter 9

The Powerful 1980s

High-heeled court shoes, power suits, oversized shoulder pads and big hair: the 1980s were all about dressing for success and living the power dream. A new breed of young upwardly mobile professionals or *Yuppies* flashed their cash as the economy boomed. Much emphasis was placed on creating an affluent image with high end designer labels branded on anything and everything.

Shoes were varied in style with the slender heeled court and slingback making the perfect accessory for the power suit. Low-heeled pumps were made popular by Diana, Princess of Wales and high-heeled shoes were the preferred style for evening. Regardless of design, it was the colour of the shoes that mattered most as they had to match the handbag and the tights. Bold fuchsia pinks, electric blues and dazzling fluorescents were

Gina red and blue leather courts, 1980s.

Seducta leather court shoes in dark metallic gold with black sculptural heels.

the hues to be seen in. The white stiletto complemented everything from dresses to leggings but created the most impact when teamed with the power suit. Towards the end of the decade, this palette of colours was replaced with gold, pewter and metallic shades as they blended well with every colour scheme.

Dr Martens were still being worn and not only by the sub-cultures but also by women who teamed these solid boots with flowing Laura Ashley dresses. However, the newest shoe statement in the 1980s was the trainer, also known as the sneaker. Although this sports shoe had been in existence since the early part of the century it was now everywhere, with people wearing them for activities other than sport. One American screen writer, director and actor famously wore a pair to the ballet while businesswomen would walk to work in their trainers, changing into their shoes when they had arrived at the office.

Vivienne Westwood

> *'Art should never be sociological; it has got to be timeless. It's got to be your vision and how you can represent the world you see'.*
>
> *Vivienne Westwood*

The first lady of fashion, Vivienne Westwood is renowned for creating innovative, quirky shoes to coincide with her equally outrageous fashion lines. One of my favourite contemporary designers, she has a talent for adding a modern twist to historical styles with the end result being rebellious cutting-edge footwear that is also quintessentially British.

In 2010 a retrospective entitled *Vivienne Westwood Shoes, An Exhibition 1973-2010* was held at the London department store, Selfridges. On display in the Ultra Lounge were some of the most celebrated examples of her work which had been amassed by a private collector over the years. Within the exhibition was a selection of the most iconic designs such as the *I am Expensive* scribble boot, the elevated *Gillies* worn by supermodel Naomi

I am Expensive Scribble boot, S/S07.

Campbell when she toppled over on the catwalk in 1993, and the bizarre pair of Mary Jane *Erotic Zones* as a nod to fetishism.

Known for revolutionary designs in shoes that shock, captivate, delight and excite, Westwood has mastered the art of creating the avant-garde. Impressive statement shoes that instantly draw the eye, they are also considered timeless classics which today are held in high esteem by those that appreciate fashion innovation as a form of art.

Westwood Biography

Born on 8 April 1941 in Glossop, Derbyshire, Vivienne Isabel Squire moved to London with her family in the 1950s. She married Derek Westwood and gave birth to a son but when the marriage broke down, she moved in with her brother. He happened to share a house with some film students and it was here, in 1965, that she met Malcolm McLaren, the man responsible for launching Westwood into the world of fashion.

Famous as the founder and manager of the punk rock band *The Sex Pistols*, McLaren joined with Westwood to open a shop, *Let it Rock* in London's King's Road in 1971. Originally selling Teddy Boy suits and rockers' gear, the shop was soon renamed *Too Fast to Live, Too Young to Die* and restocked with Triumph t-shirts, *Zoot* suits and jeans. It was during this time that Westwood began to experiment with her own designs by cutting holes and ripping up t-shirts to which she would then add chains, feathers and even chicken bones as design embellishments.

In 1974 the shop's name changed once again. Known now as *Sex*, it offered a rather more explicit and anarchic clothing range. It then became known as *Seditionaries* in 1976 which is when McLaren and Westwood made the transition into mainstream fashion with their provocative and controversial punk clothing. In 1979 the shop became known as *World's End*.

The *Pirates* collection was launched in 1981 and was to be Westwood and McLaren's first catwalk show. Sent swashbuckling down the runway with the baggy bum pirate

Pirates boots, 1981.

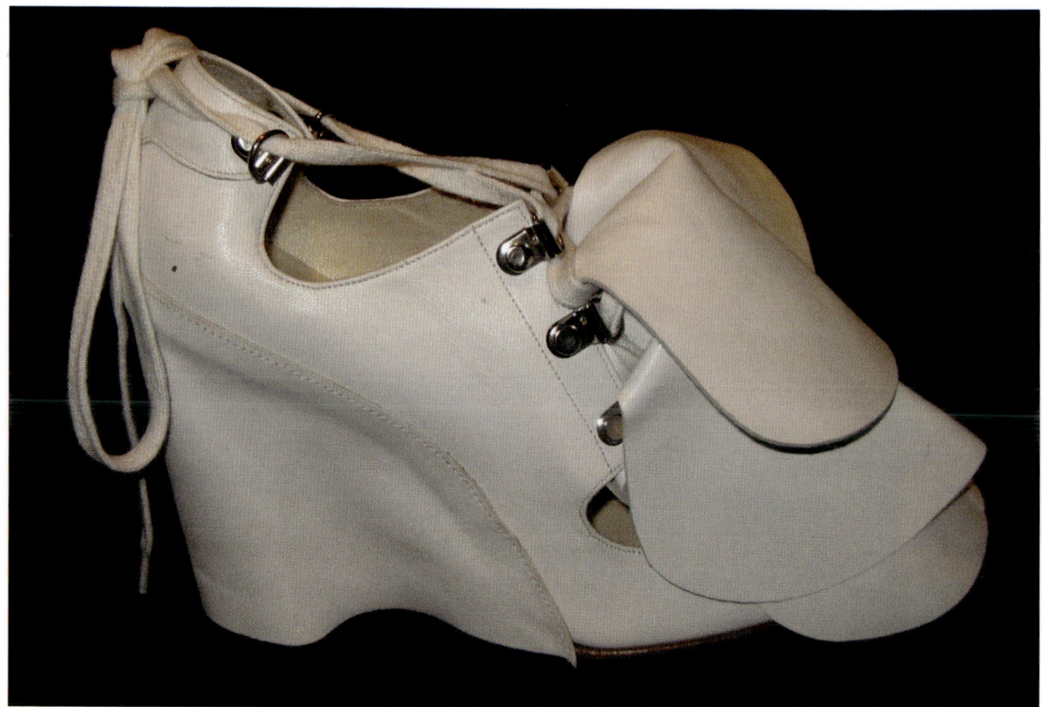

Witches three tongue trainer, 1983/1984.

trousers and asymmetrical tops were the now classic *Pirate* boots. Easily recognizable by their straps and buckles, these boots didn't originally stay in production for very long but were forced back due to popular demand years later. It is thanks to supermodel Kate Moss that the Westwood *Pirate* boot was reissued and is now available all year round regardless of season. She was photographed wearing a vintage 1980s pair she had purchased from *Rellik*, a vintage fashion shop in London, in 1999.

Due to demand from hundreds of people who wanted to possess their own pair of the iconic boots, Westwood placed them back in production. Deemed highly desirable by collectors, they are always in demand, especially if they are of original 1980s vintage with the *World's End* label stitched into the boots and the buckle shape is round instead of square; however, it should be noted that round buckles were used on reissues until 2004. It is worth purchasing a pair of modern boots with a view to them becoming desirable in years to come as these design icons are deemed legendary by shoe enthusiasts and lovers of Vivienne Westwood design alike.

The three-tongued trainer first made an appearance in Westwood/McLaren's A/W 83-84 collection entitled *Witches*. After visiting New York and meeting with graffiti artist Keith Haring, Westwood found a magical, esoteric sign language in his work which she reinterpreted into her latest collection. A trendy hip hop vibe was the styling theme, with the finishing touch being the customized trainer that emulated the freeze-frame effect of strobe lighting and the jerky beat of rap music.

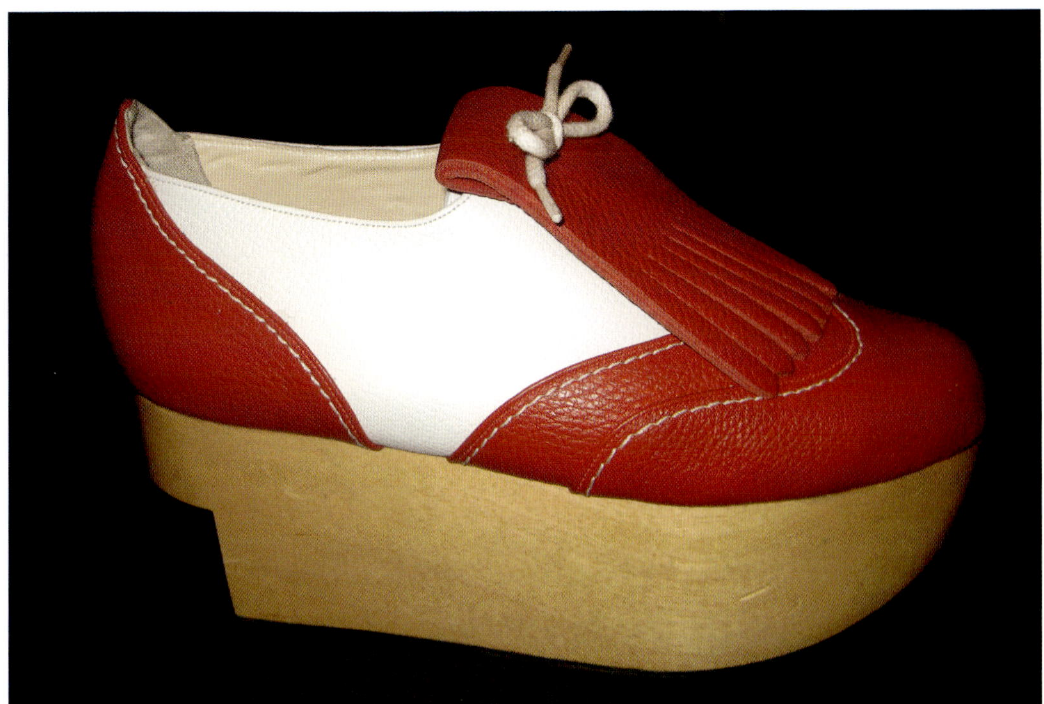

Rocking Horse shoes, 1985.

A very simple yet innovative and quirky take on the classic trainer style, this has become another desirable and sought after vintage Westwood shoe.

The *Rocking Horse* shoe became an instant collectable when it was first released in 1986.

The *Mini-Crini* 1986 collection by Westwood showcased fitted clothing, English tailoring and Princess line coats inspired by the Queen as a child. The *Petrushka* ballet also influenced this collection with Westwood's aim being to abolish the masculine big shoulders that were a popular fashion statement during this era and replace them with a doll-like look. The shoe needed to achieve ladylike poise by reflecting and enhancing the movement and sway of the ballerina-style tutu which Westwood had introduced into her collection as she believed it to be similar to the *Mini-Crini*. Shoes also had to be elevated yet comfortable to wear and walk in. The *Rocking Horse* ballerina shoe had rounded toes on a high wooden platform sole so you literally rocked along as you walked. In 1988 for the *Time Machine* collection, the *Rocking Horse*, *Golf* and *Slave* were all introduced. Today all three designs remain in production and are very much part of the iconic footwear ranges that Westwood has become renowned for creating.

One of Westwood's most famous shoes are the nine-inch high, lace up mock crocodile purple super-elevated *Gillies* worn by supermodel Naomi Campbell in the A/W 1993 *Anglomania* show. Why? Because the world looked on as the model toppled over, falling to the floor when she tried to walk in them.

Green mock crocodile super–elevated *Gillies*, 1990s.

' High Platform shoes put the woman on a pedestal like she had stepped out of a painting.

Vivienne Westwood

A direct descendent of Westwood's 1970s *Seditionaries* boots, the *Bondage* boots have become just as highly prized and respected as her *Pirate* boots. Created from leather, canvas and with moulded animal toes, the *Bondage* boot made its first appearance in 2002 for the *Nymphs* collection. In 2005 it appeared again, this time with rounded toes and the *Power Station Heel* for the *Propaganda* show. The boot continues to evolve although the main design remains the same. In 2011 it had a very high 'skyscraper' heel and in 2013 the *Bondage* boot became available in the iconic *Squiggle* print, as well as in a new colourway introduced to pay homage to the vintage 1977 boot in tan leather with green canvas.

Melissa for Westwood

Collaboration with eco-friendly plastic shoe manufacturer Melissa began in 2008 and has continued ever since. Westwood has recreated some of her most classic designs as well as completely new designs from Melissa's plastic *Melflex*™. This material is malleable, moulds to the foot and is infused with a bubble gum scent for a uniquely sweet smell. Among Westwood Melissa designs is the classic Mary Jane, fetish three-strap elevated and quirky 'winged platform' which was inspired by Alice in Wonderland and the beauty of Britain in her SS 10 collection, along with *Dragon Heart*, *Slave* and *Animal Toe*. Fun,

A collection of *Melissa Shoes* for Vivienne Westwood.

Westwood *Can* platform sandals.

stylish and inexpensive, these bold, environmentally friendly heels demonstrate how Westwood is constantly pushing the boundaries and experimenting with her innovative footwear styles.

Collecting Westwood

There are many collectors who crave Vivienne Westwood shoes since they possess all the ingredients that qualify for collectability. Quirky, innovative and basically works of art, Westwood's footwear is up there with the most desirable of shoes. Her historic vintage designs are highly sought after and her bang up-to-date modern designs are instantly recognized as fashion history in the making.

The *Pirate* and *Bondage* boots are a mainstay in Westwood's collection, as is the elevated platform shoe. Vintage and modern pairs are worth investing in as they are classics that stand the test of time.

Scour internet auction sites and general auction houses for the rarer Westwood shoes and boots as these do not come up for sale very often. I suggest buying into her new seasonal collections direct from Vivienne Westwood if your pocket allows, as this is where you can snap up her latest and limited designs that will in time become sought after.

Charles Jourdan

Even though French shoemaker Charles Jourdan began his career just after the First World War in 1919, opening his original shop in the Drome region of France in 1921, he only really came to the forefront of shoe design in the 1950s. Realising that high fashion couture shoe styles could be made at more affordable prices, he began to mass produce some of his simpler styles in different colours.

Working with his three sons who had joined the business during the Second World War, Jourdan managed to establish a brand that was a huge success. Having opened a boutique in 1957, he found that his shoes were bought by the rich and famous with the likes of Sophia Loren and Ava Gardner among his clients.

In 1959 Charles Jourdan developed a business relationship with Christian Dior and was given the licence to produce Vivier's stiletto shoes; this instantly projected him into the world of haute couture fashion. Over the years he collaborated with

White 1980s Charles Jourdan court shoes.

some of the biggest names in fashion including Yves Saint Laurent and Karl Lagerfeld. When he died in 1976, his sons continued to run the business that bore his name.

I have placed the Charles Jourdan brand in the 1980s chapter because this is when the business gained widespread international fame, with boutiques opening throughout all the major European cities and North America. Women across the globe wanted to own stylish, classically simple Charles Jourdan shoes in the 1980s and because of this many vintage pairs can be found.

Boots from the 1980s

While shoe styles were prolific during the 1980s, boots were a popular alternative. As a teenager during that decade, I remember pleading with my mum for a pair of slouch white canvas boots. My pride and joy, their only drawback was that as as I walked, they had a tendency to slide down my calf, ending up as rather baggy ankle boots!

Boots came in every length including over the knee, knee high, calf or ankle. Some, like mine, were canvas while others were leather, patent or suede. Most had some kind of same-colour piped design while others featured faux animal skin, contrasting coloured overlay patterns or two-tone shades.

Heels varied from kitten to stiletto and low block to flat. All, though, are instantly recognizable today as there is a certain distinctive look to a boot from the 1980s.

Collecting 1980s boots and shoes

'I have always loved fashion because it's a great way to express your mood. And I'm definitely a shoe lover. The right pair of shoes can change the feel of an outfit, and even change how a woman feels about herself. A woman can wear confidence on her feet with a high stiletto, or slip into weekend comfort with a soft ballet pump'.

Fergie, singer

Arola green leather boots with contrasting design and small block heel.

Yves Saint Laurent suede boots with gold leather overlay pattern.

ramel tan ankle boots from the 1980s.

Vintage snakeskin and leather red, blue and black *Panache* pumps.

Here is an era from which you can easily acquire fantastic examples of shoes at surprisingly low prices, partly due to the fact it wasn't that long ago and also because throwaway fashion was well underway by the 1980s so shoes were in abundance.

In fact this is a shoe collector's heaven as there are so many available in an eclectic mix of styles, patterns and materials. Online vintage fashion shops and internet auctions have many listings and it is also possible to unearth 1980s footwear at car boot sales and charity shops. In the past ten years, I have owned many pairs which I have worn, my favourite being a pair of black patent knee high boots with silver faux snakeskin down the sides for which I only paid £6. The truth is that not so long ago people couldn't give their 1980s shoes away but now there is a buoyant retro market for all 1980s fashion with prices very much on the rise.

Look for boots that have the piping design in bright hues or possess an unusual design. The same applies to shoes; the brighter and more characteristic of the era the better, although the same colour or two-colour neutrals are classic and look great with a corporate suit or short mini dress on a night out.

Most 1980s shoes have lasted remarkably well and turn up in good condition. You may need to get a new heel tip or sole protectors put on but this will just help the longevity of the shoe. Do avoid any pairs that have been scuffed as this can prove difficult to remove, and cracks or deep creases in leather can make the shoe look scruffy.

As with the 1970s, this is another kitsch, fun retro area of shoe collecting. Some people look back on 1980s fashion as something they experienced once in their lifetime and will never revisit. Admittedly it was pretty atrocious in some respects; I am thinking here of the Dallas/Dynasty over the top frills and shoulder pads, but when it comes to shoes there were actually some amazing designs.

Now is the right time to start buying heels from this decade, especially if you can afford some of the designer or well-known retailer names because prices are slowly creeping up. I believe that in thirty years from now they will have become rare and prized footwear fashion.

Chapter 10

The End of a Century

'*Nothing has been invented yet that will do a better job than heels at making a good pair of legs look great, or great ones look fabulous*'.

Stuart Weitzman

*T*he 1980s pretty much set the tone for the following decade and the dawn of the new millennium. Designer label footwear had already shown a significant presence throughout the previous eras but now was projected into stardom as every woman wanted and needed to own at least one pair. Manolo Blahnik, Chanel, Stuart Weitzman and Donna Karen were just some of the high-end designers whose creations were eagerly purchased by shoe savvy fashionistas. Ostentatious, vibrantly coloured shoes were no longer in vogue as black became the dominant colour, although towards the end of the 1990s vibrant hues did reappear, albeit in a rather more subtle manner.

The influence of hip hop and techno music led to the younger generations favouring sports apparel for casual daywear, completing the look with a pair of trainers, usually in the form of the new *Nike* air cushions. Towards the end of the decade the grunge subculture had travelled across the Atlantic to England; the music was inspired by heavy metal, hardcore punk and indie while the footwear of choice was, once again, the Dr Marten or any other more affordable form of *Chelsea* boot. Following on shortly afterwards into the new millennium were the emos who also have their own distinctive style which has been taken from a variety of previous subcultures. Their look involves skinny rather than baggy jeans, hooded tops and tight t-shirts. The *Converse* basketball canvas shoes known as *Chucks* or *Cons* became popular with emos, superseding the Dr Marten although

American basketball player Chuck Taylor's collaboration with Converse resulted in the brand's bestselling shoe, the Chuck Taylor All Star.

Luichiny platform boots with three dimensional red hearts.

this elasticated boot has never really gone out of fashion since its inception and is now universally prevalent, with people from all walks of life owning a pair.

And then the platform was back, just as big, bold and sometimes brazen as it had been in the 1970s.

Jimmy Choo

Like so many shoe designers before him, Jimmy Choo was the son of a cobbler who learnt the craft of shoemaking by watching his father. Born Jimmy Choo Yeang Keat in Penang, Malaysia, Choo was eleven when he made his first pair of shoes. Leaving his native country behind in the early 1980s he travelled to England to study at Cordwainers Technical College in Hackney, graduating with honours. Deciding to remain in London, in 1986 he opened his first shop in an old hospital building and within two years saw his shoes being featured in an eight-page spread in *Vogue*.

Jimmy Choo black mock croc open toe *Clue* slingback heels.

At this point Choo was operating a small manufacturing business, producing somewhere in the region of twenty pairs of shoes a week. On occasion, he would create heels for *Vogue* fashion shoots and it was because of this association that the Jimmy Choo brand was born. Accessories Editor Tamara Mellon saw the potential for Choo's shoes and suggested they partner up to create a ready-to-wear footwear range.

Princess Diana was renowned for showcasing Jimmy Choo shoes, wearing them on the red carpet at many events. The shoe designer was due to deliver a pair of gold pumps to Diana the day after she died. He kept these shoes in memory of his friend.

Opening a store in 1996 in Motcomb Street, London, the new business partners contracted out the manufacturing to Italian factories so that Choo no longer had to make the shoes himself. By the late 1990s Jimmy Choo was an international brand worn by the hottest Hollywood celebrities, and small wonder since the red carpet is the perfect runway for his shoes.

As it says on the Jimmy Choo website:

'The sexy cut, fashionable design, and exceptional Italian craftsmanship struck a chord with a sophisticated clientele and the first collection enjoyed immediate success'.

By the turn of the century Jimmy Choo shoes were being sold globally from some of the most prestigious retail establishments. But Choo didn't buy into the 'bigger is better' idea and felt the shoes lacked quality. Accordingly, in 2001 he sold his share of Jimmy Choo Ltd to Robert Bensoussan of Equinox Luxury Holdings and went back to making bespoke shoes as part of his Jimmy Choo Couture line, operating out of a small shop in Connaught Street, London.

Madonna wore a pair of Jimmy Choo's on her wedding day.

Today the Jimmy Choo brand has an empire of luxury products with shoes at its core. Its Creative Director is Jimmy Choo's niece, Sandra Choi, who first started working for her uncle at the start of his shoemaking career in the East End of London. She attended the famous St. Martin's School to study for a degree in Fashion Design while working with Choo, but abandoned her education when she realized she was learning more about the skills of cutting, stitching, fitting, designing and constructing the last from Jimmy Choo himself. Devoting her time to designing and managing the studio when the Jimmy Choo brand was initiated, Choi became Creative Director, a position she still holds today.

Jimmy Choo worked three straight days and nights sewing beads onto shoes for the Katharine Hamnett runway show.

Initially Choi 'navigated how the collection should look', continuing after her uncle's departure and also after Tamara Mellon left in 2011. She took the company beyond its stiletto–only image by introducing a broader range of shoe styles and designs.

Although the shoes are no longer designed by Jimmy Choo himself, you could say that a part of him still lives on in the current ranges as his niece, who learnt her art from Choo, is at the helm of the creative side and has been instrumental in taking the brand to a new and excitingly luxurious level.

Stuart Weitzman

'I design shoes that make women happy'.

Stuart Weitzman

Red suede pump displaying a gold metal heel by Stuart Weitzman.

Rita Hayworth was the inspiration behind Stuart Weitzman's most unique collection of shoes. The peep toe *Sienna* satin heels in chocolate brown (a colour usually alien to Weitzman's designs) displayed a satin flower on each shoe which cradled an earring of diamonds, sapphires and rubies that belonged to Rita Hayworth. Worn by the actress in the 1994 film *The Shawshank Redemption*, the shoes were priced at $3 million and are considered the world's most expensive shoes.

Weitzman has used a wealth of unconventional materials in his shoe designs including wallpaper, diamonds and gold.

As with so many other famed shoe designers, the shoe business is ingrained in Weitzman's family. His father was a shoemaker who opened a factory in Massachusetts called *Seymour Shoes* during the 1950s. At the age of sixteen, Stuart Weitzman went to the factory and sketched his first shoe design; the design was duly produced and today it has been bronzed as a reminder of what Weitzman describes 'as a rudimentary beginning of my shoe creativity'.

After spending time creating shoes for his father's label, when Weitzman Senior passed away, Stuart and his brother Warren took over the business. The brand was sold in 1972 to a Spanish company but Weitzman continued to design their shoes and purchased the company back as soon as he could.

Weitzman red *Moc Croc* slingback heels, 1990s.

Stuart Weitzman's first inspiration is the woman who is destined to wear his designs, his goal being to create a shoe that will make people smile, and that people will remember. He states that the 'binding element is that there is something special in that shoe.'

Weitzman shoes from the 1990s have been described as 'minimalist perfection' and in the 2000s he has created some of the most undisputedly magnificent heels for celebrities. Actress Laura Harring wore his platinum sandals adorned with 464 diamonds for her appearance at the Oscars in 2002. More controversially, in 2007 Weitzman created *Retro Rose*, a fabulous pair of shoes embellished with one million dollars' worth of diamonds, for *Juno* screenwriter Diablo Cody to wear to that year's Oscars ceremony. The controversy arose from the fact that Cody chose not to wear them, opting instead for a pair of gold sandals from her own wardrobe. Despite having to face a backlash for her decision, Cody was unrepentant and defended herself by saying she wasn't aware she had to wear them to the ceremony.

Exquisite yet sometimes eccentric, Weitzman heels are gallant designs that are adored by women throughout the world due to the glamorous femininity they instantly bestow on the wearer.

Christian Louboutin

> *'Shoes are just a pedestal. What interests me is the power of the woman who wears them'.*
>
> Christian Laboutin

Those distinctive blood red soles that we have come to instantly associate with the shoe creations of French-born shoemaker, Christian Louboutin first appeared in the 1990s and have remained as the definition of glamour ever since their inception.

The inspiration for those trademark outer soles came in 1993 when Louboutin saw his assistant painting her red nails. He told *Footwear News*: 'I thought, oh my god! Red soles are so flirtatious.' Intending to use them just for that season's collection, when his customers asked him to continue with the new idea they became Louboutin's signature soles.

'The shiny red colour of the soles has no function other than to identify to the public that they are mine. I selected the colour because it is engaging, flirtatious, memorable, and the colour of passion.'

Christian Louboutin's distinctive red soles.

On a visit to the Musée des Arts Africains et Océaniens, the young Louboutin noticed a sign on the wall that had a woman's pump shoe crossed out with a red line, indicating that high heels were not allowed as they damaged the wooden floor. This image stayed with Louboutin who found it fascinating and it possibly became the catalyst that set him on his incredible shoemaking path.

Louboutin defends his designs from fakes or copiers. He is famed for taking Yves Saint Laurent to court over that fashion house's use of red outsoles identical to his own.

The idea of creating fantastical footwear began when Louboutin was a teenager. Frequenting the theatres and music halls of the time, the French designer was drawn by the eclectic mix of personalities and the bizarre yet sensual environment. Having been expelled from school at sixteen, he came up with the idea of making shoes for the dancers and started to sell them direct to the theatres. Louboutin went on to work at the famous Parisian cabaret Folies Bergère where he once again created stunning shoes

Christian Louboutin *Luggage* shoe in the Bata Shoe Museum, Toronto.

Louboutin black patent sky-high heels.

for the dancers. Then, in 1982, he took employment with Charles Jourdan where he learnt every aspect of shoemaking.

Working as a freelancer for a while, he fashioned shoes for Yves Saint Laurent and Chanel before founding his own Parisian house where he set about designing his own collection of dangerously high but sexy heels.

Music legend Madonna was instrumental in introducing Louboutin shoes to the world as she wore his heels in her videos.

Classic Louboutin *Very Prive* heels in rose.

Louboutin's inspiration is drawn from a variety of eclectic sources including the arts, landscapes, popular culture and even astrology. His 2016 *Zodiac* collection of satin shoes, detailed with astrological symbols woven in gold and silver thread and available on two iconic Louboutin shoes styles, the *Rocket Flat* and the open toe *Akenana Mule*, could be personalized on the red sole with the owner's initials and date of birth to 'ensure the shoes are as unique as the woman wearing them'. Only forty-five pairs were available, sold exclusively by online luxury fashion retailer *Moda Operandi* to celebrate their fifth anniversary.

Classic signature Louboutin shapes like the *Pigalle*, which launched in 2004 with its sharply pointed toe, and 2006's *Very Prive* with open toe and hidden platform, are often used as blank canvases for more flamboyant designs as Louboutin is a master of experimentation, using unusual embellishments and materials.

Long tassels, plumes, spikes and plastic googly eyes, there are some really wacky Louboutin heels that convey a sense of humour yet still radiate a sexy feminine silhouette.

'High heels are pleasure with pain'.

Christian Louboutin

Green slingbacks with stacked ball heel by Italian shoe
designer Andrea Pfister.

Vivienne Westwood super-elevated blue
Gillie platforms worn by supermodel
Naomi Campbell.

Considered the crème de la crème of sky-high designer heels, whether richly embellished or clean stylistic designs, each one is a unique and beautiful creation. Christian Louboutin is a designer that sees no boundaries but also appreciates the sleek sophisticated silhouette of an elegant shoe, creating heels that encompass everything a woman doesn't necessarily need but absolutely wants.

Collecting the 1990s

I have mentioned just a few of the most desirable high-end luxury designers from the 1990s but there were many more including Prada, Mark Jacobs, Andrea Pfister and Gucci. It goes without saying that if you can buy into the 1990s' designer shoe market then you are investing well, especially if you can unearth the more unusual designs. It is possible to pick up some well-known designer shoes from this decade really reasonably on internet auction sites. However, there is an abundance of other names in shoes from the 1990s that really epitomize the era and are perfect for starting a collection. Look for high street offerings from the likes of Hobbs, Shellys, Faith, Clarkes and Dolcis. The *Red or Dead* label by Wayne Hemmingway was really big in the 1990s and you can find some fantastic examples on the secondary market.

Supermodel Naomi Campbell famously toppled over on the catwalk in 1993 when wearing a pair of Vivienne Westwood super-elevated blue mock croc *Gillie* platforms.

Geri Halliwell of the Spice Girls famously wore the 1997 Shellys *Union Jack* platform boots which have become instantly recognizable as a 1990s fashion icon. It is possible to find a genuine pair of Shellys *Union Jack* boots which sell for around £75 but there are many other ankle and knee-high 1990s platform boots out there to snap up for your collection.

Chapter 11

The New Millennium

Footwear design has progressed rapidly over the years with the twentieth century contributing considerably to this growth. Today shoes are far more than protective forms of footwear as, aside from making a visual statement about social grouping, personal tastes and status, they also showcase the talents and capabilities of the designers who compete to produce the most innovate displays of creativeness in their designs.

Continually pushing the boundaries, the designers create pure masterpieces in footwear and this creativity is not restricted to the high-end luxury market. The high street is crammed full of innovative, eye-catching shoes and then there are the bespoke designers who produce one-off designs that are literally works of art. The main consensus for the footwear fashion of the new millennium is that basically anything goes, from the most simple styles to the positively outrageous. Every colour, design and shape is acceptable as

Andrea Pfister's pineapple print cowboy boots with pineapple-shaped heel, 2002-2003, for *Carmen Miranda* collection.

is each form of covering and embellishment. Various textiles, animal skins, Perspex and mesh with finishing touches of sequins, beading, precious stones and even gold all add extra kudos.

A plethora of styles and designs in the twenty-first century have rocketed a new breed of designers into the limelight. Some have made a massive impact on the fashion scene and are commercially established where others remain designers whose avant-garde, cutting-edge creations are works of art or in, some cases, 'literally out of this world' shoes.

Alexander McQueen

> # '*I find beauty in the grotesque, like most artists'.*
>
> *Alexander McQueen*

A pure genius and innovator of ground-breaking fashion collections, the late Alexander McQueen set the fashion world alight. Outrageous, dramatic and extravagant, his designs often shocked and amazed as McQueen was a master of theatrical showmanship, ensuring that his fantastical collections in both clothing and shoes always took centre stage.

Tragically, McQueen took his own life by hanging himself in his wardrobe with his favourite belt on 11 February 2010. Having achieved immense respect for his great achievements in British fashion, McQueen is sadly missed by those that appreciate his sublime ability to produce ground-breaking collections by thinking 'outside the box'. Constantly wowing the fashion savvy with controversial and often dark displays in his runway shows, McQueen made captivating fashion statements which is why he has left behind a unique and avant-garde legacy.

Born in the East End of London, Lee Alexander McQueen left school at sixteen to embark on an apprenticeship at Saville Row tailors Anderson and Shephard. Afterwards he joined Gieves & Hawkes, the celebrated tailors to the royal family since 1809.

He later joined theatrical costumiers *Angels and Berman* who have been dressing the entertainment industry since 1840, when the founder Morris Angel opened a second-hand clothing shop and hired out clothes to actors. This is without doubt where McQueen fell in love with theatrical drama which soon became evident in his own collections. After spending time at the company mastering six different methods of pattern cutting, from the historic sixteenth century techniques through to contemporary tailoring, McQueen took employment with Koji Tatsuno, a Japanese designer who at the age of nineteen came to London on a buying trip for an antiques dealer and never returned. He, too, believes in

Overleaf: Alien shoes, Alexander McQueen, 2010.

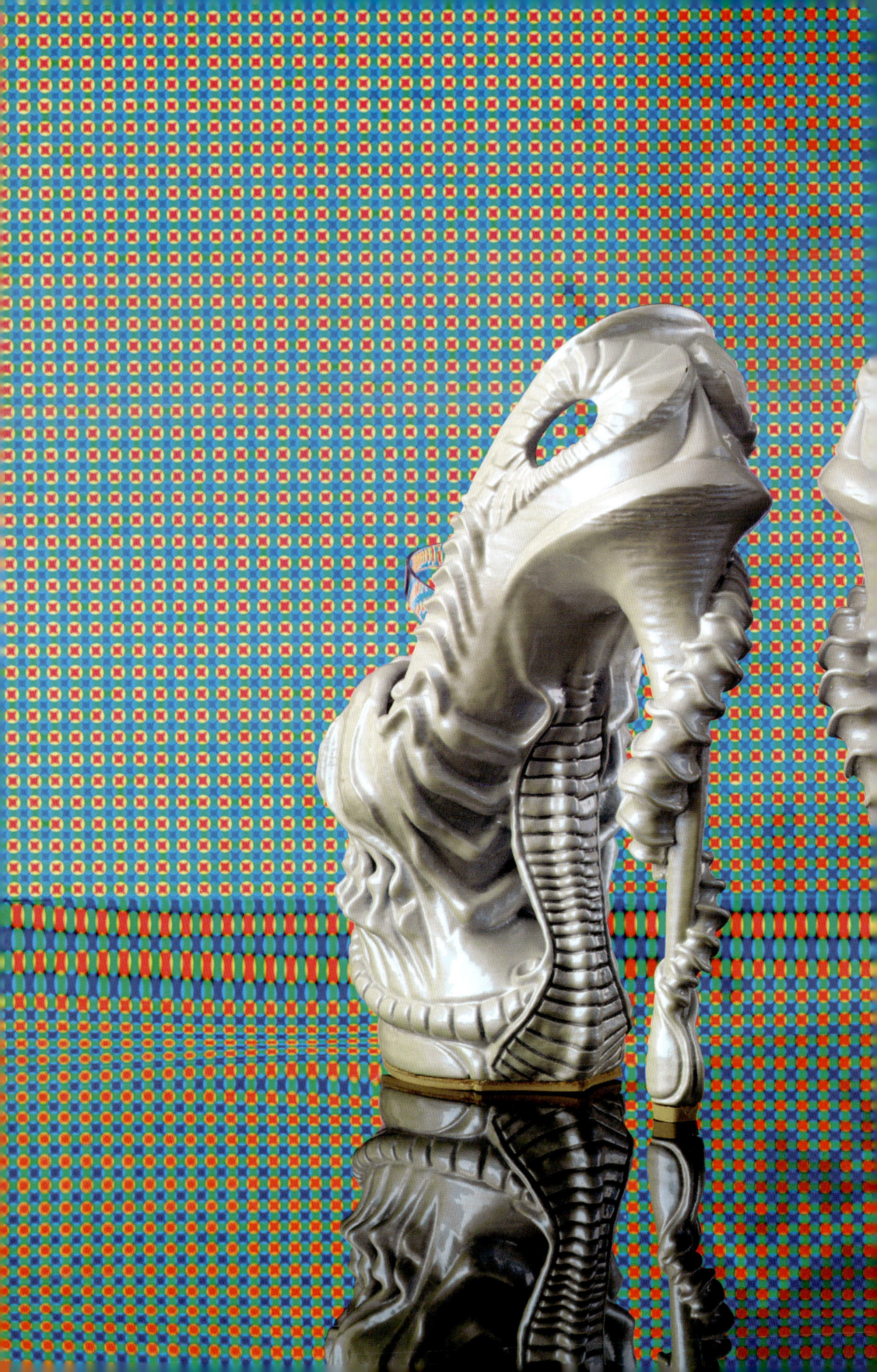

Monarch Butterfly thronged
sandals, 2011.

Gold Iris ostrich feather
boots, 2001.

shock tactics in his clothing designs and it is probable that they influenced McQueen's own fashion initiatives.

After a year, McQueen travelled to Milan and spent time employed as a design assistant before returning to London and enrolling at the Central Saint Martins

McQueen designed the wardrobe for David Bowie's tours in 1996–1997 as well as the famous Union Jack coat worn by Bowie on the cover of his *Earthling* album.

fashion college where he completed a Master's degree. In 1992 he showed his graduation collection which was inspired by Jack the Ripper. The entire collection was by Isabella Blow, magazine editor and muse of hat designer Philip Treacy. As a result, McQueen suddenly found himself catapulted into fashion stardom.

After graduating, McQueen set up his own label in the East End of London and then in 1996 he was appointed Head Designer at French fashion label Givenchy, following in the footsteps of John Galliano. When his first collection was unsuccessful, McQueen toned down his designs but he still kept his distinctive, rebellious streak alive, causing controversy in 1998 when double amputee model Aimee Mullins strode down the catwalk on carved wooden legs. One year later his show presented a model in a white dress rotating on the catwalk while two robotic guns blasted her with neon paint.

In 2001, feeling that his creativity was being constrained, he left Givenchy and immediately sold 51% of his own label to Gucci where he felt his talent was encouraged rather than suppressed. Now the way was clear for Alexander McQueen's fashion house to become an international success.

With a reputation for being an *enfant terrible* due to his frequent outbursts and petulant bad boy image, McQueen was still held in high regard and loved by all in the fashion industry. His runway shows continued to electrify with his creations reflecting his own personal rebellious side. This unique fashion edge was evident in his clothes and dramatic shows as well as in the outrageous, bizarre and ground-breaking shoes that adorned the models' feet.

McQueen received the award for British Designer of the Year no fewer than four times (in 1996, 1997, 2001 and 2003) and was Men's Designer of the Year in 2004. He was also honoured with a CBE, presented by Her Majesty the Queen in 2003.

Artistic sculptures on ridiculously high heels, the shoes played a pivotal role by adding the dramatic final touch to McQueen's ensembles. Colliding fashion and art, these heels were visually breath-taking as well as being ingeniously empowering. Weird yet wonderful, the shoes captured the essence of the theme of his shows with a repeating trend of being completely crazy and not of this world. They were, literally, show stopping heels that would be a tall order for any woman to walk in.

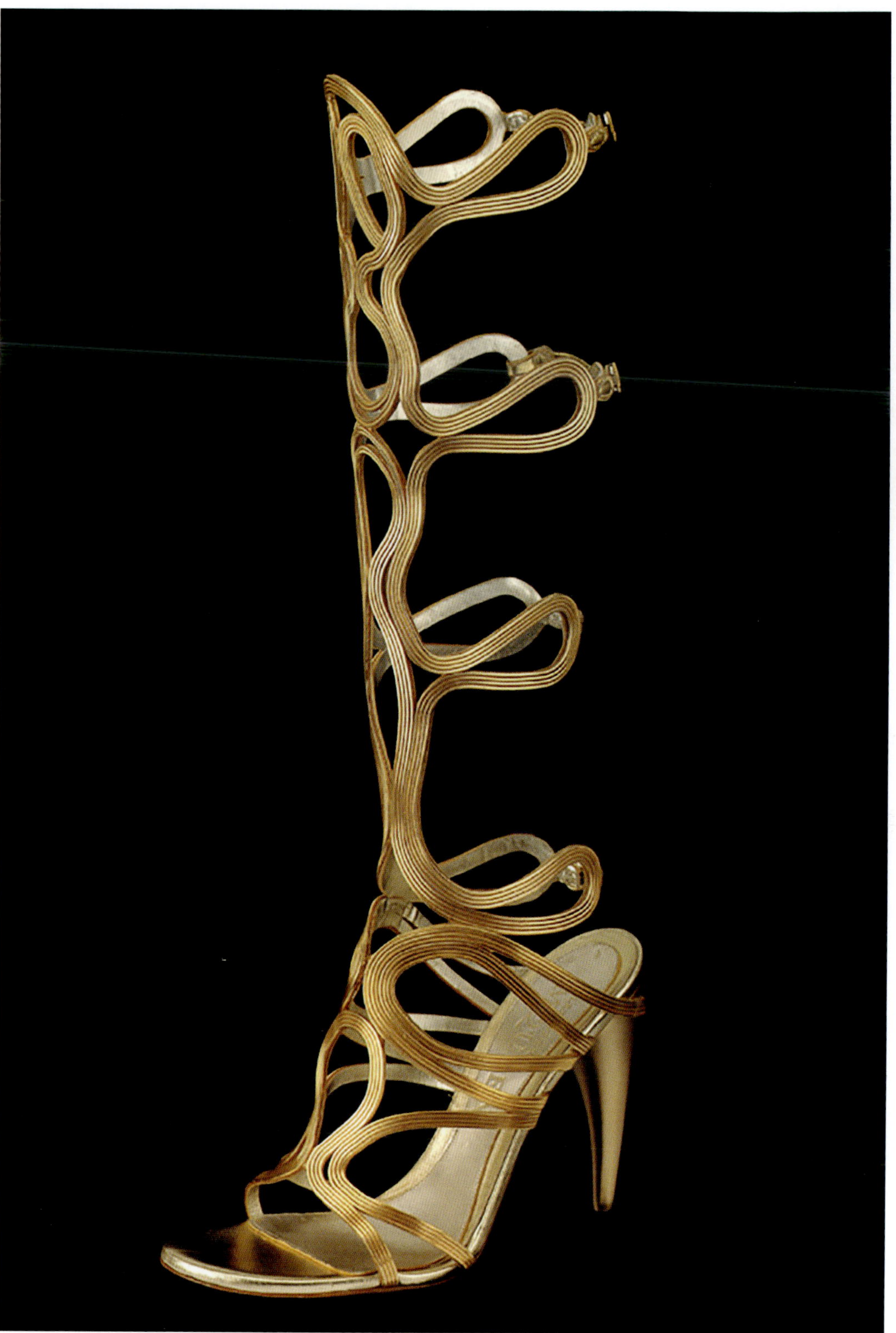

Neptune boots, 2006.

Armadillo Hoof boots, 2010.

In Memory of Elizabeth Howe, part of the collection which paid homage to one of McQueen's distant relatives who was hanged during the Salem witch trials of 1692.

The first pair to really hit the headlines was the *Armadillo Hoof* design which McQueen showed in his Spring 2010 *Plato's Atlantis*, show based on Charles Darwin's *Origins of Species*. His models apparently refused to wear the extraordinarily high *Armadillo Hoof* heels for fear of safety; however, pop icon Lady Gaga had more courage, famously sporting the boots with their twelve-inch heels in her *Bad Romance* video. Daphne Guinness, meanwhile, was the first celebrity to grace the red carpet wearing a nude pair.

Apparently only twenty-one pairs of the *Armadillo Hoof* boots exist. They originally retailed at between $3,900 and $10,000 a pair depending on style, skin and embroidery. McQueen was quoted as saying about the heels: 'The world needs fantasy, not reality. We have enough reality today.' Fantastical they certainly are since they are practically impossible to walk in, yet these were the heels that made the world realise McQueen should also be taken seriously as a talented shoe designer.

Collecting Alexander McQueen
Since his tragic and untimely death in 2010, McQueen's creations have become even more sought after by both collectors and fashionistas. As a result, the market value for anything with his name attached has been pushed upwards. McQueen was an innovator of fashion and his runway shoe designs were sculptural works of art rather than understated classic. Renowned for pushing the boundaries, his shoes are quirky and outrageous with the zip front *Skull Heel* ankle boot a recent signature design for his brand. When a great artist passes, their work instantly gains recognition on the collectors' market and this is exactly what has happened with all of McQueen's fashion lines, including the shoes. Already highly desirable, these shoes are snapped up the minute they go on sale and it's a safe bet that they will rocket in value. The ultimate investment heels, they should go on to command thousands of pounds in the future.

Nicholas Kirkwood

British shoe designer Nicholas Kirkwood creates towering architectural heels that are sculptural visions, incorporating unique materials into his designs. Laser cut mirrored leather, shaved stingray, lacquered aluminium and rubberized suede have all featured in his shoe creations so it should come as no surprise to learn that he has won a number of prestigious awards for his design innovation.

Kirkwood began his fashion career while studying a foundation course at Central Saint Martins. On a skiing holiday in 1999 he met the milliner Philip Treacy who offered Kirkwood work experience in his shop. Kirkwood accepted and ended up staying with Treacy for the next five years. Kirkwood soon realised through the customers he encountered that there was a gap in the market for statement shoes and so he enrolled at Cordwainers, the shoemaking college. Once he had learnt the art of shoe making he dropped out of his studies and returned to work with Treacy.

Trying to raise money to design his own collection, Kirkwood produced shoes for John Rocha and Ghost's catwalk shows. When his eponymous collection was launched in the spring of 2005, it set the wheel in motion for his career as a shoe designer. Collaborating with Rodarte, Peter Pilotto, Erdem and Prabal Gurung, Kirkwood also produces his own collections season on season which include statement heels as well as more conventional, classic shoe shapes, all of which possess that trademark hint of sculpture.

Kirkwood concentrates on the innovation of form rather than decorative elements. His heels are about clean lines and geometric silhouettes but he does get to 'play' more with the shoes in his collaborations.

Kirkwood for Rodarte *Sand Shoes* featuring dripping wax heel.

Rodarte and Kirkwood heels

Kirkwood has for many years collaborated with Rodarte, a clothing and accessories brand. The A/W 2010/11 collection saw Kirkwood design shoes with little LED lights in the heel that glowed through to give a dripped wax effect. The *Sand Shoes*, released in 2010, were again innovational with red suede straps, leather sides with cut out detailing, leather tie ankle straps and, their pièce de résistance, a five-inch PVC heel which resembled dripping wax. With only a handful thought to be in existence and each pair retailing at just over £1,000, these covetable heels are definite future museum pieces that showcase genius design elements.

Kirkwood for Liberty *Bounty* heels.

Danny Sullivan and Irregular Choice

'It does not matter who the woman is, they all love to have a pair of "WOW" shoes in their wardrobe'.

Funky footwear doesn't get much more exciting than that created by the hands of Danny Sullivan for Irregular Choice. The fantastically bizarre yet completely mesmerising designs capture everything that a shoe obsessive wants and needs. Offering everything from sculptural heels and fabulous fabrics to kooky shapes and originality in design,

Irregular Choice.

Irregular Choice is the new footwear phenomenon that has taken the high street by storm.

Beans on Toast, Ball and Chain, Frilly Knickers and *Juicy Gossip* are just a very small selection of the shoes you will discover when delving into the wondrous world of Danny Sullivan's Irregular Choice footwear collections. Showcasing stylish yet positively unique designs, there is a shoe or boot to satisfy even the most jaded of shoe enthusiasts. An array of styles, variety of materials and extravagance of embellishments ensures that every wedge, pump, court and stiletto-heeled shoe proudly displays a unique visual treat that draws the eye of anyone fashion forward enough to appreciate quirky individualism.

Early days

Sullivan was always destined to be a shoemaker since both his parents created crazy footwear throughout the 1970s, 1980s and 1990s. Reminiscing about childhood memories, Sullivan talks of how he often found himself subjected to his mother and father talking fashion and shoes around the dinner table. He also spent much of his youth being dragged

Release the Unicorn.

around trade fairs, shoe factories and retail stores where he would be stuck in a corner waiting patiently while his parents attended meetings.

It was while on one of these business trips, visiting the factories in Italy, that Sullivan sketched his first shoe design:

'I (very badly) drew a shoe whilst sitting in the back of the car. My parents loved it so much they actually placed the design into production'.

In fact many of Sullivan's early designs were so impressive that they made it to the manufacturing stage.

After leaving school aged just fifteen, Sullivan began to learn the art of shoemaking from his parents. With no formal training they enhanced their skills through trial and error; shying away from conformity, the family developed their own distinctive styles in footwear which Sullivan believes is why their designs are so different from more conventional shoemakers.

Danny Sullivan believes that if he hadn't been a shoe designer he would still have been involved with something quite artistic. With a passion for furniture and lighting, this might have been his alternative design path.

Some years later Sullivan left home to seek an alternative career path but he soon returned to his roots. Shoe designing was the only thing he knew and loved and as a result, aged twenty-eight in 1999, he founded Irregular Choice. Since then he has never looked back. His parents now live in China but are still very much a part of their son's growing shoe empire; his mother creates all the samples while his father looks after the production side.

Beans on Toast in a metallic leather of red and black stripes with a carved wooden heel; the scarlet lining adds the finishing touches to this exquisite design.

Almost twenty years since the inception of Irregular Choice the brand is going from strength to strength. With thousands of faithful followers all desperate to acquire the latest season's offerings, Sullivan is constantly under pressure to come up with fresh ideas in shoe design.

Gaining inspiration from literally anything and everything, Sullivan feels that it is all about how you perceive things. For example, a group of people might look at the same item but then each of those people might see it differently. Sullivan likes to observe everything from a fun, cute and irregular way which he then transports into his shoe designs as he believes this is the essence of what Irregular Choice is all about.

Initially Sullivan will sketch an idea, making it as clear as possible so that his vision can easily be explained to his colleagues. Next comes the making of the lasts, followed by the heel and, finally, Sullivan will consider the patterns and materials that will work best with the design. Fabrics are a very important part of the shoemaking process for Sullivan as he loves the diversity of colours combined with the variety of patterns and textures.

Innovation in heel design is one of the areas Sullivan likes to experiment in; this pair of *Juicy Gossip* shoes showcases how Sullivan is successful in producing eccentric, stylised designs; the heel is a gold gem-shape attached to a suede shoe with an elegant ankle strap secured by a popper and tassel trim.

> '*I often see people wearing my shoe designs and every time it gives me a real buzz but nothing compares to the first time I saw a random person wearing a pair at Waterloo Station in London. It was like a first love or first kiss, this memory still holds a special place for me*'.

Sullivan also enjoys working with wood for heels and platforms as it lends itself well to experimenting with interesting shapes and angles. Trying to find a balance of creating something out of a compound or material that is workable for production is the most important aspect. One of the hardest and most unusual heels Sullivan ever created was from small stacked pieces of wood that curved round. He explains that normally you would need a metal pin to go down through the centre of the heel in order to take a person's weight but in this instance the pin was removed so that the heel could be curved. It was then stacked with a number of small pieces of wood. In theory this design shouldn't have worked but with determination Sullivan was successful in proving to everyone who refused to believe in it that if you put your mind to something, then anything is possible.

Pushing the boundaries of conventional shoemaking by experimenting with every process from the inception of the design to the finished article, Sullivan's shoes speak eloquently about his design skills. When his visions become reality, the result is truly innovative and exciting footwear.

Collecting Irregular Choice

Irregular Choice is already pretty high on the collector's radar with people desperately wanting to own the latest collections or eagerly seeking those shoe designs which are no longer available. Some tend to concentrate on just buying as many Irregular Choice shoes as their budget will allow while others cherry pick their own personal favourite styles.

The other compelling reason for collecting this brand is its affordability. Being able to purchase kooky, elaborate designs that are still produced to the highest standard for

London College of Fashion Irregular Choice shoes.

considerably less than your average designer label shoe attracts collectors to Danny Sullivan's footwear like bees to a honeypot.

One of the most talented shoe designers of the twenty-first century, Sullivan recognizes that women of all ages and from every walk of life love to own innovative show-stopping shoes. So it is no surprise that this high street brand has fast become highly coveted. Funky footwear at its best, Irregular Choice shoes are destined to become future investment pieces as an ever-increasing number of women fall for the label's quirky, fun designs.

In 2011 Irregular Choice launched a limited edition London College of Fashion collection as part of the student design project. Competition was fierce, with only two talented students, So-Yeon Sarah Ahn and Rosanna Gault winning the coveted prize of having their unique designs placed into production and sold by the footwear company. The selected shoe designs reflected world cultures and architectural utopias with a playful twist which married perfectly with the ethos behind the Irregular Choice brand.

A combination of heart-shaped sculptured heels, candy cane stripes, ditsy florals and oversized bows and feathers, these quirky design-led shoes managed to be on trend while maintaining the idiosyncratic sense of style for which Irregular Choice is famed.

Olivia Rubin for Dune

Olivia Rubin is one of the hottest new British designers to emerge onto the fashion scene in the twenty-first century. Adored by celebrities, her distinctive graphic print dresses in refined, feminine silhouettes have been featured regularly in glossy magazines and snapped up by faithful followers of fashion. Rubin possesses a talent and aptitude for design which is reflected throughout her stunning clothing ranges and, more recently, in her debut range of shoes produced exclusively for the luxury footwear retailer, Dune. For her striking and bold collection, Rubin transported a selection of her show-stopping signature prints onto Mary Jane pumps, vintage 1970s-inspired wedges and raffia platforms. Gaining instant acclaim from shoe enthusiasts with an eye for design innovation, Rubin has ably demonstrated that she is a young designer who deserves to be taken seriously.

The limited edition capsule collection released in spring/summer 2011 consisted of twelve shoe designs which were exclusively available through Dune retail outlets and the Dune concession in London's Selfridges department store. From bang on trend, brightly coloured prints to pastel abstract patterns the collection mirrored a selection of Rubin's earlier SS10 and AW10 clothing collection which had been inspired by iconic contemporary artists. Taking the colour palettes from the artists' great works, Rubin reinterpreted them onto her über-stylish shoe range which included a Matisse

Warhol Raffia platform; Andy Warhol was famed for his pop art screen printed imagery of famous icons such as Elizabeth Taylor, Marilyn Monroe and the Campbell's soup tin, and now his vibrant colour palette has been recreated by Rubin on her raffia platform shoes which are as full of artistic merit as Warhol's prints.

wedge, Warhol and Dali raffia platforms, a Monet pump and a Picasso Mary Jane. By devising this innovative and clever way of infusing art with fashion Rubin has, like the other inspirational shoe designers within the pages of this book, proved that footwear is indeed an art form which can be as blatant or as subtle as the designer chooses to make it.

This 1970s-style *Matisse* wedge has a slingback strap and bow detail on the toe which adds a touch of elegance; revamping her SS10 curve print, the young designer rescaled the original to produce a contrasting colour palette, opting for this ensemble because she wanted something soft and neutral.

Rubin's progression in design

Rubin was always destined to work within the arts as from an early age it was apparent that she possessed artistic flair inherited from her grandfather who was a prolific painter. Spending endless hours drawing and painting, Rubin was encouraged at school to develop her talents and was introduced by one of her teachers to the skill of screen printing. This art form tied in perfectly with Rubin's other passion for textiles and fashion so it wasn't long before the young designer had replaced her drawing with designing and creating fashion illustrations.

Dali raffia platform; taking inspiration Salvador Dali's surrealism, Rubin designed this stunning platform in vibrant shades of blue, pink, green and black.

On completing her studies Rubin continued to pursue her chosen career path as a fashion designer. Fascinated by the industry and what it had to offer she enquired at the Central Saint Martins College of Art and Design concerning a course she had become aware of on John Galliano. However, she actually ended up applying and being accepted for the foundation course of *Creativity and alternative ways of dressing.*

Rubin's natural flair and talent for fashion design ensured she graduated from the college in 2006 with a BA in Fashion Print. Her final collection was shown at the Annual Press Show and received much attention from the national press, with the London *Evening Standard* newspaper citing her *Naked Body* print as one of the standout collections.

In 2000 when Rubin began working for couture designer Jacques Azagury she learnt the skills of pattern cutting and embroidery designs for the fashion label. She then went on to find work placements with two of the most iconic and theatrical designers of our time, the late great Alexander McQueen, and John Galliano who is renowned for his fantastical designs. Rubin's potential certainly didn't go unnoticed by these designers as her print designs were chosen by McQueen for his AW05/06 menswear collection as well as the pre-fall womenswear collection for the same season. Galliano, meanwhile, developed Rubin's talents in all areas of fashion including working on lingerie lines and accessories as well as embellishing and sampling. She also assisted backstage on Galliano's mainline shows and the Dior haute couture show; this was an exciting experience and one where Rubin felt most at home as she loved the buzzing atmosphere behind the scenes.

Rubin's fashion career continued to flourish and then in 2004 she was employed on a freelance basis by the *All Saints* clothing company as an embroidery and print designer. She also worked alongside Tristan Webber in the run up to his SS05 London Fashion Week show, as well as designing for Jade Jagger's *Jezebel* collection in SS08. However, it was when her first collection was released under the Olivia Rubin label in 2007 that the spotlight's full beam hit her, making her one of the most exciting new designers

The print on this *Emin* peep toe court derived from Rubin's AW10 *Mono* print which had a darker edge than most of her other collections and was inspired by raindrops; by juxtaposing the strong, graphic design Dune's classic, 'pretty' shoe shapes such as peep toes and Mary Janes with bows, Rubin created the perfect balance between harsh and soft.

to appear on the fashion scene. Both her SS07 and SS08 collections were shortlisted for the *Fashion Fringe Award Scheme* which instantly gave Rubin the platform to exhibit her designs at London Fashion Week.

AW09 saw Rubin's first highly anticipated catwalk show in association with the *On/Off* catwalk shows and designer exhibition at the Science Museum in London.

Since the inception of the Olivia Rubin label there has been no looking back for this refreshingly innovative designer. Constantly working on collaborations for both her clothing and her accessory lines, Rubin has become a name synonymous with young, cutting edge fashion. Using only the best materials and ensuring that her ranges are of the highest quality, Rubin is constantly inspired by fresh new ideas which she first sketches before developing them into wearable fashion lines.

Inspiration is gained from a variety of sources which are both creative and personal. Sometimes a design idea will derive from the most mundane object or vision, and sometimes from the most awesome. For instance, her signature *Brick* print which appears in every season's collection was simply inspired by a building site which Rubin walked past every day for a month.

Being a determined young designer, Rubin is driven by creativity as well as a burning ambition to succeed. So with her fashion label going from strength to strength it seemed only natural for her to diversify into creating a range of shoes and accessories. Dune had always been strong supporters of Rubin's work so when they decided to embark on their first ever designer collaboration there was no doubt that she would be heading up the venture. Working as a team they created an exciting range of shoes, matching handbags and pashmina scarves. Rubin described the collaboration as an 'incredible experience as the collection had something for everybody.' Jamie Brogden, Head of Design at Dune, was also elated with the collection and stated that:

> *'Dune were thrilled to be launching their first designer collaboration with Olivia Rubin, who is one of the most dynamic and recognized young British designers'.*

As well as marking a new and exciting direction for Dune, the exclusive range confirmed that Rubin really is one of the hottest new designers of the twenty-first century.

Collecting Rubin's Dune shoes

When it comes to the important business of collecting Olivia Rubin fashion lines there are already many followers that, like me, appreciate that her graphic clothing designs are destined to become highly sought after in years to come. So you can imagine how excited both shoe enthusiasts and collectors became when they realised that she was launching an exclusive range of shoes in collaboration with Dune. These show-stopping shoes, produced as limited editions, designed by a reputable designer and available for a limited period, the shoes were like catnip to the fashion conscious.

Collectors are always drawn to shoes that combine a designer name with artistic quality and limited availability. Where Rubin has the edge, however, is in the fact that her shoes are not only wonderful stylised works of art but also completely wearable. Olivia Rubin is a British designer who is destined for great things. Soon to become desirable pieces of fashion history, her designs are sure to be wise investments.

Picasso Mary Jane; Rubin's tribute to the great Pablo Picasso has been recreated on a Mary Jane shoe with slender heel and button bar.

Maï Lamore

'A shoe, more than any other clothing item, is an object that already exists before even being worn'.

Extravagant opulence are the words I would use to describe the stunning high-heeled couture creations by Parisian shoe designer, Maï Lamore. The elegant forms embellished with feminine trimmings of feathers, jewels and gold along with tactile satins and silky skins represent every woman's 'guilty pleasure' as they are an indulgence of sheer luxury.

Breathing life into her shoe designs, Lamore transforms practical footwear into magnificent artistic sculptures. The exquisite *Rose* shoe created from hand dyed silks, gold and precious stones and the quirky *Black Panther* sandals in silky shaved mink are just examples of how this designer has rocketed shoe design to a higher level. Placing her heart and soul into every shoe, Lamore is a true artist who is in a permanent state of inspiration as everything she sees, hears, reads or experiences inspires her work, resulting in outstandingly lavish creations that every woman would wish to own.

Born in Bangassou on the banks of the Oubangui River in Central African Republic, Lamore explains that much of her childhood was spent growing up in a magical land. The breath-taking scenery, the play of light between the forest galleries and the savanna, and the extreme contrast of the violence of the tropical storms with the burning silence of the dry season: these all contributed to Lamore's diverse and thrilling outlook on life. She remembers how the heart of the forest provided an idyllic place for reading her classic books while listening to music as diverse as that of Mozart, Wagner, Georges Brassens and Aretha Franklin. At night, the sky enabled Lamore to contemplate the immensity from which she would draw her own constellations. All of these experiences of natural beauty set the scene for Lamore's future in design, as a sense of naturalism is reflected in all of her creations..

However, Lamore's incredible childhood experiences did not solely stem from her beautiful naturalistic surroundings but also from the wonderful thoughts that filled her mind. Both her parents embraced the mysteriousness of a magical life and would share elaborate secrets and memories with

Lamore's father owned a coffee plantation while her mother was creative in designing furniture for the home as well as dresses for herself and her daughter.

Leopard shoes; a bizarre yet totally workable design of
a leopard whose outstretched limbs create the toe strap
with its tail trailing after the back of the heel.

Panther shoes.

their daughter, of people and times passed. One particular story was that Lamore's grandmother was a queen who wore sandals made from gold pieces set with jewels. Lamore explains that for her the inherited mysteries and the upheavals of this period created such an impact on her life that she poses herself as the heiress of these worlds, the values of which she has continued to employ within her fashion designing because, in her own mind, it is a deeper and far richer universe.

Angel's Dew is a romantic name for an incredibly romantic shoe design; a platform heel that possesses a nest of Lesage embroidery, this stylized killer heel also features a crystal and gold chick.

Artistic beginnings

Lamore first became conscious of the skills and talents that would eventually lead her into a successful fashion career while attending boarding school in France. Upon completing her studies, the young designer returned briefly to Africa before setting up life back in France where she gained employment as the director of boutiques and later a consultant for the development of collections. Constantly impassioned by design, Lamore was responsible for designing the *African Queen*, one of the first restaurants to merge design with culinary arts. She then went on to successfully open three contemporary art galleries in the Marais area of Paris and founded *Mamba*, an avant-garde magazine where she became Director of Publication. Along with being the initiator and director for some of the world's most important cultural projects, working together with the French Ministries of Culture, Foreign Affairs and the Department of Culture for the City of Paris, Lamore has throughout her career collaborated with international museums and prestigious exhibitions around the globe which have included retrospectives of African photography.

Prestigious shoes

It was Lamore's obsessive passion for shoes that eventually projected the designer into fashion stardom. Having worked for six years as a creative director for women's footwear brands in New York and Japan, Lamore felt she was being held back by the economical imperatives dictated by a commercial luxury shoe line where creativity was often opposed. So, in secret, she began to develop her own line of luxurious haute couture shoes. Her aim was to elevate women's footwear to a standard of high luxury and she achieved this by designing prestigious shoes that can be placed in triumph upon a woman's foot.

All of Mai Lamore's haute couture shoe lines exert a magical power on those that wear them, as they are sculptural works of art that epitomize elegance, femininity and sensuality. Attention to detail is paramount as each shoe, whether it is the left or right, receives the same level of intricate detailing, thus ensuring that no aspect of the refinement is neglected. With shoes made from the most opulent materials such as satin, silk and shaved mink, and lavishly decorated with gold, pearls and semi-precious stones expertly set by a master jeweller, it follows that only the most affluent women are able to afford Lamore's luxurious heels.

This level of intricacy from the inception of the design to the decoration of the shoe is a domain traditionally reserved for haute

It took twenty years for Lamore to finally launch her stunning shoe designs onto the market.

Lamore initially sketches or paints her shoes designs in watercolour. She also creates small model master sculptures in wood or bronze.

Above and Opposite: Sentiment Profound rose shoe is a thing of beauty which should be admired as an art form and has a price tag of £17,197; the petals are created from hand dyed silk, the thorn heel is of 18ct gold and a bee resting on the shoe is produced from gold, onyx and agate.

couture fashion pieces that adorn other parts of a woman's body. However, Lamore has broken the mould and projected the art of shoe design into another dimension and this has ensured her place as a thus-far totally unrivalled master in the industry of haute couture shoemaking. Footwear that shouldn't simply be worn and admired but seriously considered as exceptional works of art, Mai Lamore's designs are every fashionista's holy grail.

Lamore has designed a prêt-a-porter collection that is inspired by the more upmarket luxury haute couture designs yet is more affordable, with a price tag of £1,400 upwards. Although less expensive than her couture range, these shoes reflect the talents of this artistic shoemaker as they possess sculptural heels and the unique traits which are synonymous with Mai Lamore's more luxurious designs.

Above and Overleaf: Peacock Feather shoes completely embellished with hand-dyed feathers ensure that the wearer will stand as proud as a peacock when beautifying their feet with these spectacular shoes.

Annejet Kosters

'*Let the shoes influence the wearer in an eccentric way, both physically and mentally*'.

Annejet Kosters

Experimental shoes are the forte of Dutch designer Annejet Kosters. Combining quality, design and function she creates fantastical footwear which only the most extremely fashion forward would wear on their feet. Typically high art, these shoes merge divine with torturous and brilliance with unorthodox as they are stunning to behold yet unconventional in style. A young designer who stands out in a league of her own, Koster creates shoes that instantly catch the attention and I strongly believe they are the epitome of just how far twenty-first century design has advanced.

Visually tempting and intriguingly practical, Kosters' shoes can be front-less, as in her *Golden Heels*, have innovative detailing as displayed in the *Marilyn Monroe*

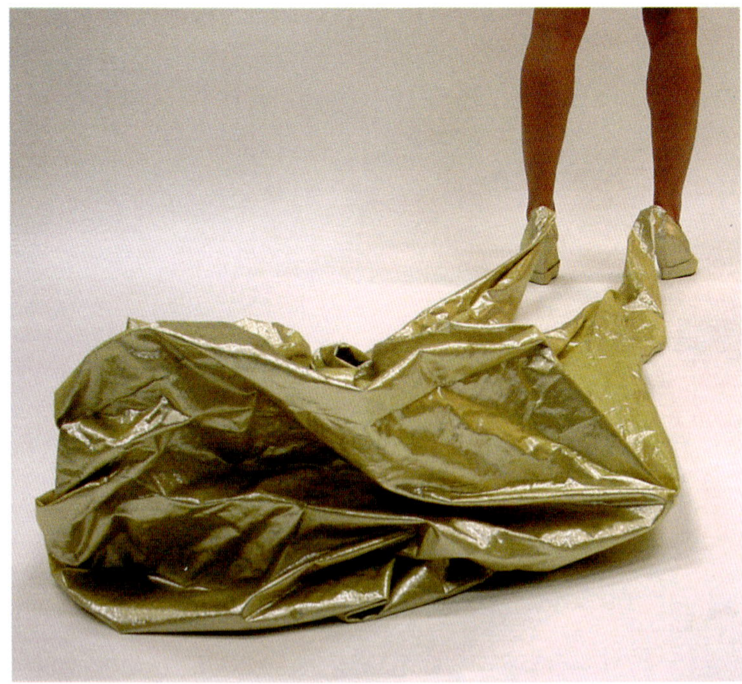

This outrageous pair
of wedding shoes most
definitely falls into the
artistic category of footwear;
created from both textile
and leather, the left and the
right shoe are attached to
each other by one and a half
metres of long train, and
Kosters states that striding
on these shoes makes the
wearer feel aware that at this
moment in life she is walking
away from her past into the
direction she chooses.

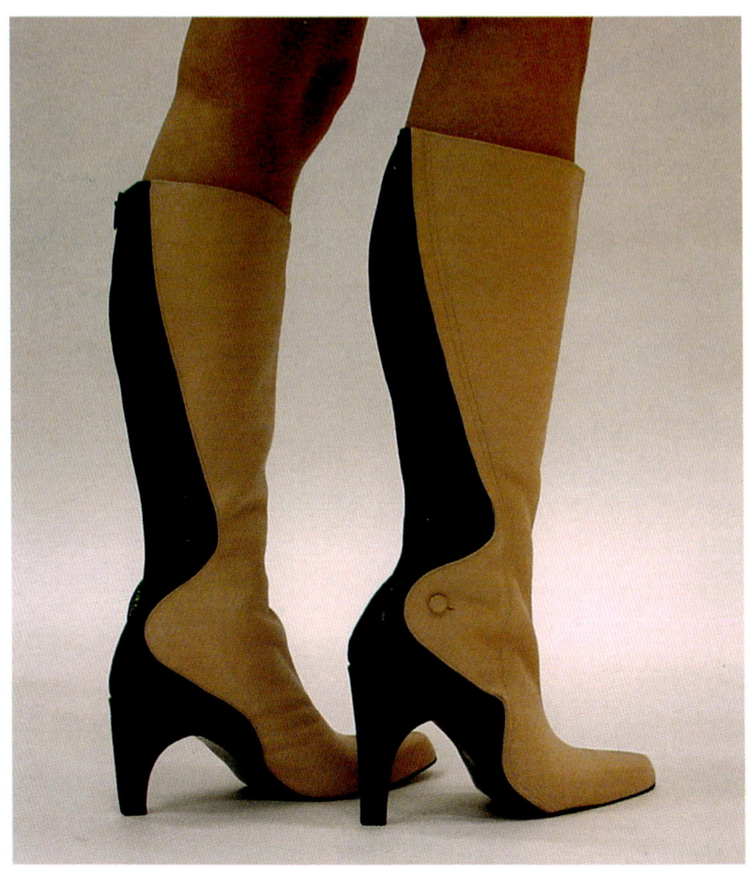

Monroe boot with heels of
different heights which
results in the wearer swaying
her hips as she walks.

boots and feature kooky concepts as depicted in her *Wedding* shoes. Taking an idea and imprinting her own artistic stamp on it, Kosters designs footwear that is not for the fainthearted but it is guaranteed to bring out the extrovert in all those that have the courage to wear them.

Design development

Born in 1981 in Utrecht, the Netherlands, Annejet Kosters developed a passion for shoes at a very young age. She remembers manipulating and assembling her own unique shoes by attaching blocks under her ballet pumps to create heels, then embellishing them

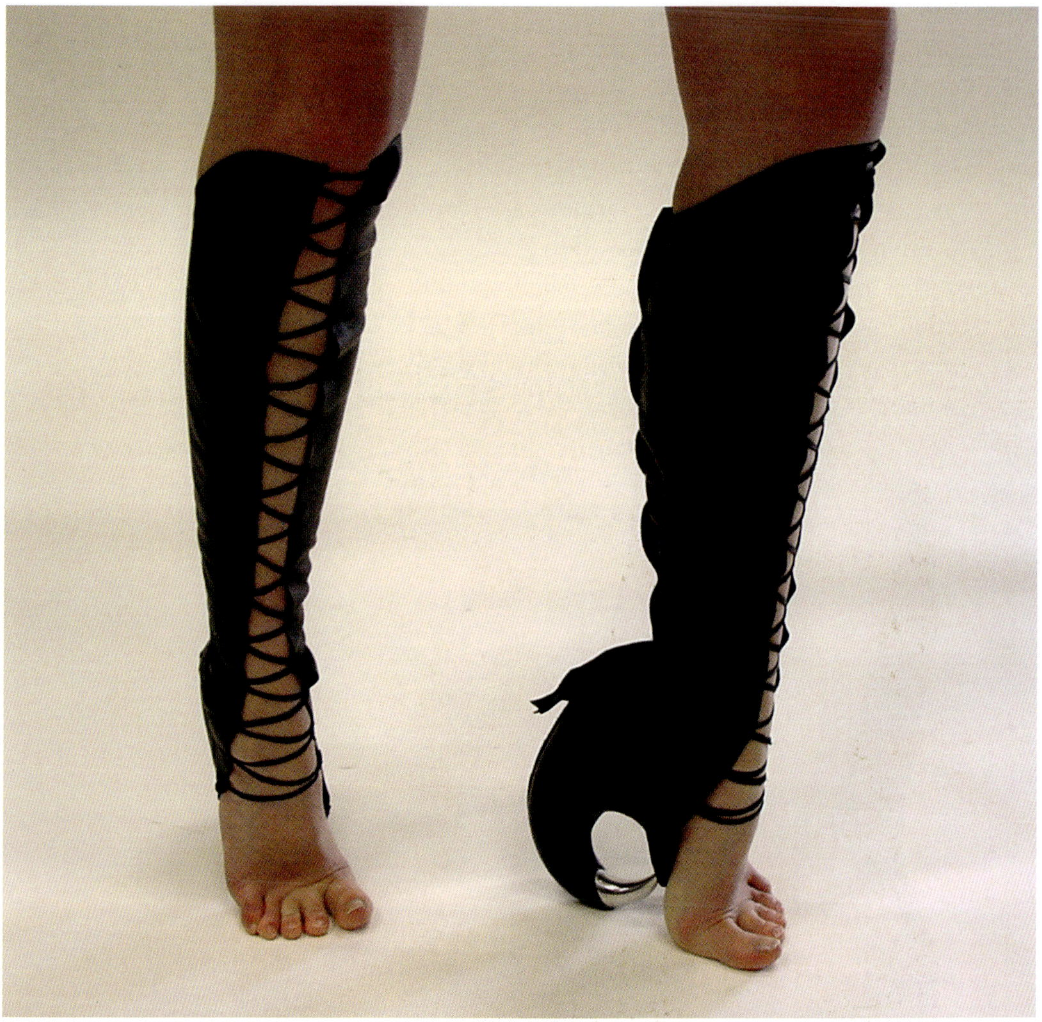

Kosters created *The Billy* shoes, a revolutionary design in which the high heel bends back to the arch and then tries to stick into the foot, from leather and aluminium; while I am unsure whether I would risk wearing these shoes as the aluminium spike looks painful, my hat goes off to Kosters for creating such futuristic and really rather erotic footwear.

with all kinds of girlie handmade decorations. This initial deep yearning to design was something she nurtured right into her adult years.

Originally studying Product Design at Art School for a year, Kosters realized that the subject was too broad and wanted to find a specific area in which to specialize. With a love for shoes and a fascination for the tension created by their function and beauty, shoe design was an obvious choice. So, in 2001 Kosters decided to complete her education by enrolling on a three year course to learn the art of handmade shoemaking.

By 2004 the young designer had graduated from the Utrecht College of Arts with a Major in 3D Product Design as well as a degree in Handcrafted Shoe Design. Her final graduation collection entitled *Lady Utopia* has been described as bringing both amazement and wonder to the wearer as well as to the observer because each of these experimental handmade shoes has a completely unique image. Kosters explains that the initial concept for creating this collection was to let the shoes influence the wearer in an eccentric way, both physically and mentally. The common factor is that the shoes influence the movement of those that wear them, making them saunter, stride or sway their hips, with a subtle performance as the end result.

This unique approach to shoe design ensured that once Kosters had completed her studies she was easily able to gain employment on a freelance basis within the commercial sector, in addition to continually experimenting with her own personal shoe designs.

Kosters believes that walking on bare feet and simultaneously having the experience of wearing high heels is sensational.

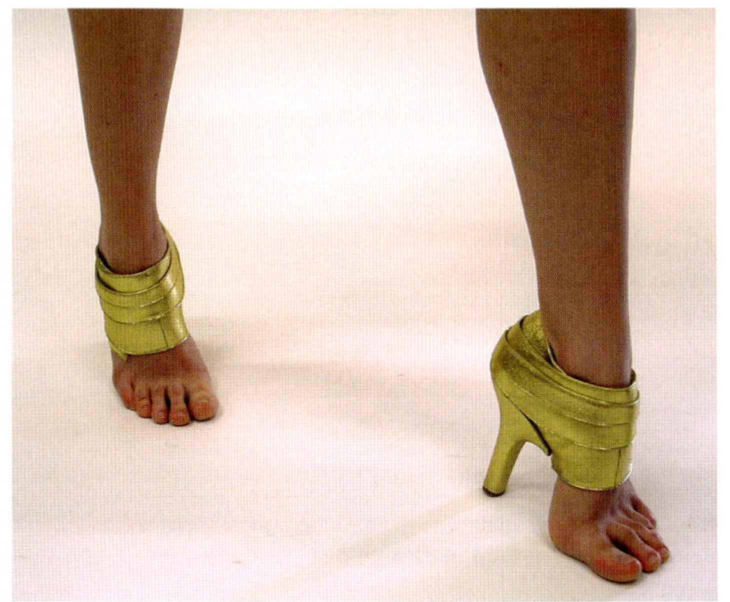

Kosters, whose *Golden Heels* exemplify the young designer's unique use of the foot as part of the design, describes these particular shoes as jewels for the feet; the metallic golden leather is tightly wrapped several times around the instep, exposing the foot and the toes, while the heel gives balance, letting the wearer experience the sensation of walking in bare feet and in heels at the same time.

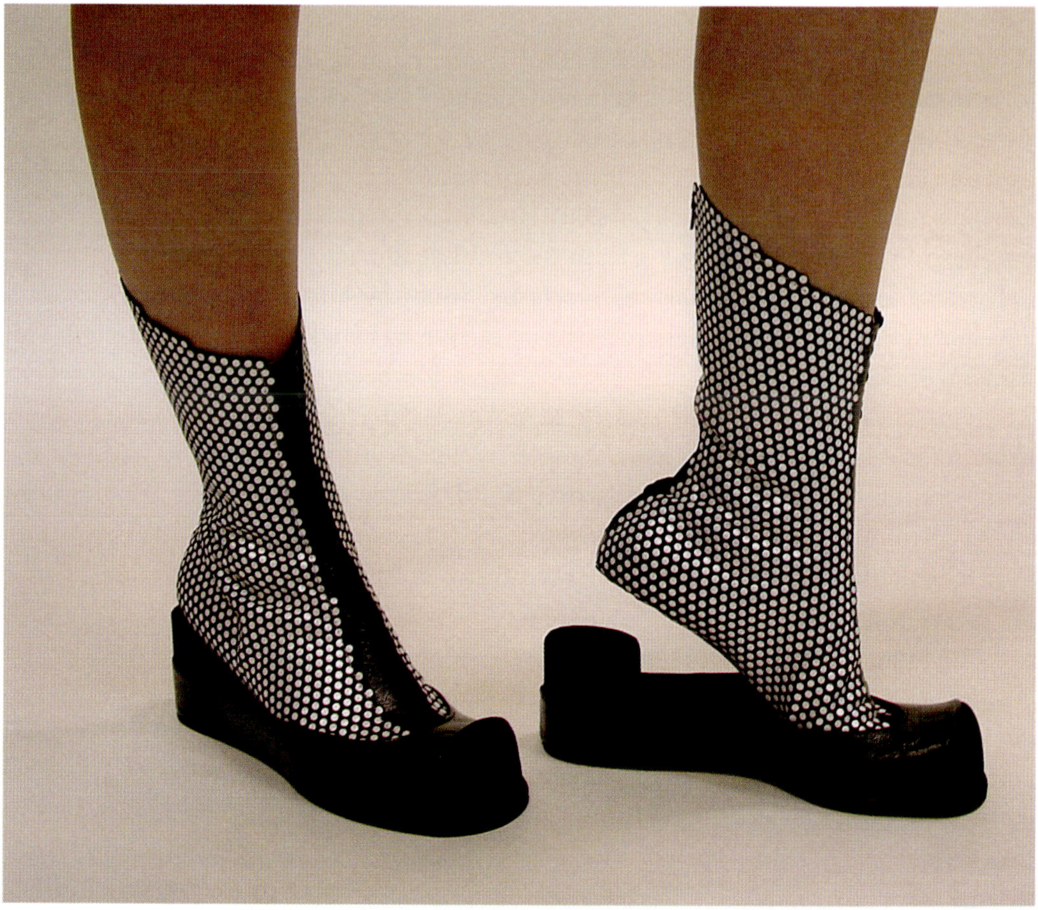

Making a clapping sound when worn, the *Clap* shoe combines artistic design elements with the demands of practical footwear; an unconventional design which has the heel attached to the top of the shoe results in the *Clap* shoe making a clapping sound when worn, rather like the noise made by flip flops.

Producing beautiful yet functional footwear has always been an essential factor in Kosters' work as she realizes that these are two of the main elements which satisfy customer needs. She achieves this by gaining inspiration mainly from social observations although this young designer also has an eye for three-dimensional shapes and aesthetic detailing. Colour plays an important role, as do high quality and using sustainable materials, so by implementing all these factors along with balancing technique and trends, Kosters is able to produce seriously artistic designs in shoes.

Collecting Kosters

Since Annejet Kosters is a design artist who produces one-off shoes, at the present time it is impossible to collect her quirky, adventurous footwear. However, I did feel she needed to be featured in this book as the *Lady Utopia* collection is one of the most staggeringly innovative shoe collections I have ever encountered.

This young designer has more than proved herself worthy of being considered one of today's most talented shoemakers. I strongly believe that anyone with an affinity for adventurous shoes should keep a watchful eye on Kosters as she is sure to become a highly celebrated designer in the not too distant future.

Kobi Levi

'When I design a shoe I think about it as a sculpture to wear, an art piece you live with'.

Those seeking quirkiness in shoe design need look no further than the extraordinary footwear created by Israeli designer Kobi Levi. Bridging a fine line between fashion and art, his shoes are so outrageous that only the most adventurous of style-conscious women would be able to carry them off with the credit they deserve.

Most people would never consider wearing a pair of banana skins or shopping baskets on their feet but Levi makes this bizarre concept a reality as his 'crazy' shoes are inspired by everyday objects, foods and animals. Wearable works of art, the extrovert styles are a clash of practicality and surrealism, with an added injection of humour.

The inspiration behind the Banana shoes came about when Levi started to consider that when a shoe meets a banana skin on the floor it usually ends up in an accident; so instead of slipping on a banana these are banana slip-ons, created from leather with a rubber tread on the bottom to make sure the wearer will certainly be noticed.

Levi's life

Levi's passion for art began at an early age; he was always drawing and sculpting so his parents gave their full support for his career choice. In high school, he studied the arts and felt that for some reason he always created 'shoe-related' pieces. He remembers being given a piece of wire for a three-dimensional assignment with the instructions that he was to create a sculpture from a single line. Moulding the wire with no cutting is the most limiting form of art as the designer needs to concentrate on the shape as it evolves. It should come as no surprise that Levi created a high-heeled shoe sculpture which could be opened at the back for a foot to be placed inside.

To further his education within the art world, Levi attended the Bezalel Academy of Art & Design in Jerusalem. Graduating in 2001, he specialized in the development,

These stylized *Aluminium* shoes came about when Levi was studying metal ware in college; experimenting with aluminium casting techniques while the rest of his class were casting sculptures, Levi was creating various heel designs with the object of creating a heel with fluidity and a shape with movement.

making and design of footwear. Working as a freelance designer, he has over the years collaborated with both Israeli and international companies on varied assignments including creating a shoe line for men and designing industrial footwear. Alongside producing more commercial ranges Levi, has for his own pleasure, been designing his 'crazy' shoes. Currently only one-of-a kind pairs, his ambition is that one day everyone will be able to own a pair of his shoes with the ultimate accolade being celebrities adorning their feet with Kobi Levi footwear.

Levi's unconventional shoes are born from a visualization in his mind; this could be a concept, an image or a theme. He then explores the possibilities and turns those visions into reality. To achieve this, the process of creating just one pair of shoes can take Levi as long as a month to complete. He begins with sketching the idea from a number of different angles and, once happy, he will then work on a three-dimensional skeleton prototype. The next step is selecting the materials with which he wants to work. Leather, textiles, rubber, wood and even metal are all considered but Levi has to choose the ones that will give the

Kobi Levi studied the making of jewellery and accessories at college and as a result has also designed unusual quirky handbags, one of which is in the shape of a toaster.

Chewing Gum sneaker; this crazy but brilliantly executed design came about when Levi wanted to 'freeze' a moment in time; having explored the concept that high heels are like walking on your toes, he merged this idea with a sports sneaker, resulting in a 'sport elegance' design that gives the impression of the chewing gum being the heel although it can also be interpreted that the heel is not actually a part of the shoe.

desired effect and also will work best for both the technical elements and the design itself. He is also conscious that the material should behave, as any mistakes in the design process will mean he has to start from scratch. Modelling them by hand, the shoes begin to evolve although Levi explains that he never really knows exactly how the footwear is going to look until it is completed and it really comes 'alive.'

Levi explains that when he designs a shoe he thinks about it as a sculpture to wear, an art piece you live with:

> 'You and your body affect its look and it affects yours. Footwear should have its life with and without being on the feet, on the contrary to clothes that exist only when being worn'.

Passionate about design

Levi's shoes have an individuality which projects immense personality. Humorous and quirky but most of all fun, they are bold statement pieces that represent perfectly how fashion and design have positively collided. From the innovative *Banana* shoes to the complex *Miao* and the sex-fuelled fantasies of the blow-up doll, entitled simply *Blow*, to the sinuous lines of the architectural *Aluminium* heeled shoes, each represents a unique insight into just how any everyday object or vision can be easily translated into footwear.

Collecting Kobi

As mentioned previously, at the moment many of these shoes are one-off prototypes so collecting them is nigh on impossible unless you are in the fortunate position of being able to commission Levi to make a pair especially for you. However, such

Levi's dream is to see his shoes worn by pop and style icons and he also hopes to collaborate in the future with fashion designers.

is his talent that I believe he is a designer of whom we are going to see a lot more in the future, and as he grows so will the collectability of his designs. Levi's shoes border on the bizarre yet also slot into the twenty-first century eccentricity that is such a hot trend at the moment. Individualism, standing out in a crowd and getting noticed is what fashionistas crave but these are also the qualities that collectors adore. His shoes possess

Levi designed the *Miao* shoes after witnessing a stray cat stretching and realising that this imagery was perfect for a shoe design as cats are very fluid and elegant in their lines; these shoes were the hardest Levi has ever designed as it was all about building the inner three-dimensional shape to simulate the cat silhouette and movement.

all the right ingredients as they are outrageous, fantastically designed and unique. Kobi Levi's work is already receiving much publicity and hype which suggests that the stage is set for his shoe designs to become iconic fashion favourites in the future.

All of the above-mentioned shoe designers are expressing art through fashion, creating heels that make a statement, yet all are completely wearable. However, I wanted to finish this book with a bang by showcasing an artist whose shoes would make you gasp at the sheer craftsmanship. Shoes that can never be worn in the practical sense as they are sculptural pieces of art but represent the true sinus and powerful form of a stiletto.

Recently I had the great privilege of meeting with Kobi Levi in London. He placed some of his shoe designs on the table in front of us and I was able to witness the stir they caused, with women stopping what they were doing to admire and discuss his work.

Contemporary Chinese combines Chinese culture and art imagery with a western high heel stiletto; the red and gold upper is inspired by a fierce fire-dragon but this intensity is balanced by a light and minimal double stiletto chopsticks heel.

Omar Angel Perez

'As an expression of appreciation, I offer my gratitude to all women who endure the torture of wearing such heels. Your sacrifice does not go unnoticed'.

Omar Angel Perez

Only the very bravest fashionistas would ever consider wearing a pair of Omar Angel Perez's accentuated spiked *Stilett'O'* heels, and even then the art of walking would probably prove impossible. This is because Perez is not a conventional shoe designer

Omar and Lindsey.

but a very skilled and talented artist who has embraced the form of a humble shoe and masterfully created sky-high heel sculptures.

Perez's playful pieces explore the sadistic world of any fashionista's shoe fetish; a series of forms expertly crafted from a variety of materials, they encompass the elegant structure and stylistic design of a true stiletto shoe. Although not wearable footwear in the practical sense, I refuse to believe that any woman would not have their breath taken away and their inner desires awakened by the sheer presence of these works of art in shoes.

Perez's path to design
Born in Houston, Texas in 1963, Perez was probably always destined to pursue a path in the arts as both his parents were creative. His father handmade most of Perez's childhood toys and his mother worked as a gifted painter and seamstress.

Perez studied Fine Arts and Graphic Design at the University of Houston from 1981 until 1985 when he graduated with a B.F.A. Ever since, Perez has established a reputation of being a true artisan in the world of woodwork craftsmanship.

Specializing in making and crafting furniture, Perez frequently exhibits his work which has become widely admired and eagerly collected. He has undertaken many public and private commissions including the *Tectonic Tango* hall table and the *Heliosentry* sculptural hall cabinet. He has also exhibited in prestigious institutions such as the American Craft Council Show and Houston Centre for Contemporary Craft.

Azzurra, 2010.

Bat Girl, boot, 2009.

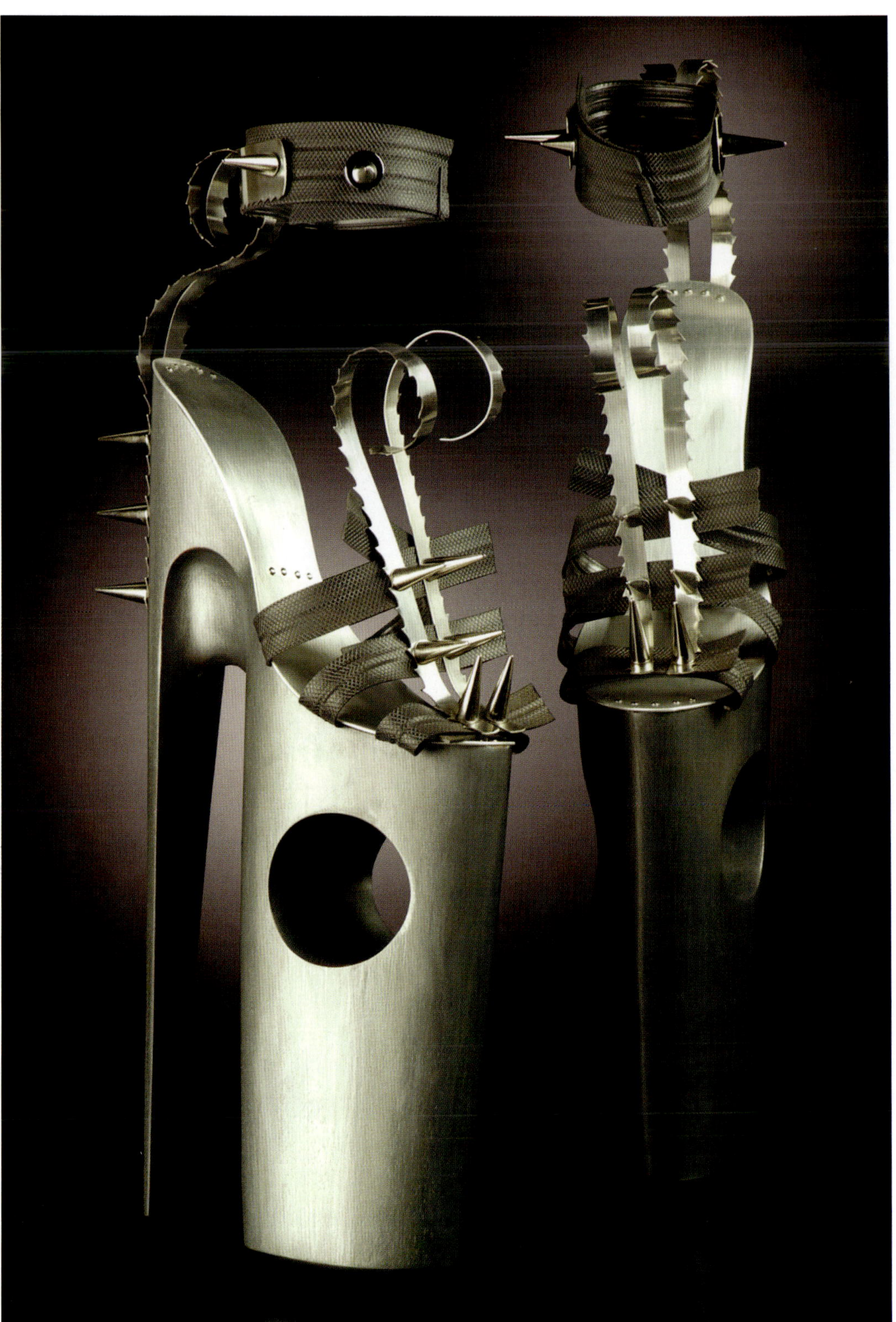

Dystopia.

Inspiration is taken from a mixed palette of cultures, fashions and even foods, all of which guide Perez along his creative path. Reflected in his pieces are juxtapositions of various woods, colours and materials from all around the world which result in a playful, sexy drama. Perez tells 'how these antics are an invitation to engage and touch'.

> *'I am blessed that I find design in everything around me, yet sometimes this is a curse in that I am forced to take the time to examine every angle, curve and shape of those surroundings'.*

The colour, the texture, even the smell of exotic woods is intrinsically beautiful to Perez, as they provide a virtuously endless palette from which to choose. He believes that the rare woods bring not only vibrant colours but also a richness of burls and dramatic figures to his work. His biggest challenge is being able to complement the wood's natural beauty by creating a vessel that is expressive.

Stilett'O'
The famed Stilett'O' heels first came about in 2009 as a bit of a joke. Perez was constantly being teased by co-workers and friends about his tendency to look at a woman's shoes and legs before noticing her face. As a result, he decided to make a pair of sculptural heels to join in with the joke:

> *'Everyone laughed when I presented my first shoe but after letting the fun settle most really appreciated the craftsmanship and design'.*

These heels offered Perez an amusing way to experiment with materials and since the inception of the first shoe, his fantastical footwear designs have gained great interest and credibility among those that appreciate fine sculptural art. Receiving much press attention with rave reviews, the collection of sky-high heel sculptures has been exhibited in the *Omar Angel Perez: Stilett'O'* exhibition.

Like a Virgin.

My Shoes are Killing Me are words many women can identify with when walking home barefoot, carrying their high heels, after a night of dancing; inspired by stories of torture, Perez created this shoe as tribute to all those women who choose beauty over pain with the heel symbolizing this perfectly as the beauty of the rosewood and makore is paired with the threatening bandsaw blades; while Perez can still not understand why anyone would pay so much money to walk on a pair of stilettos when they will inevitably cause discomfort, I believe you have to be female to realize the answer to that one.

Trust No One apparently is your shoe of choice should you find yourself spying undercover in a drug cartel; you should look 'all together' in your expensive lizard heels yet underneath the façade, your weapon of choice is a bullet, hence the term 'killer heels'; the title of this shoe came to Perez when he was applying a dollar bill as embellishment to the shoe, and noticed on the back that it read 'In God We Trust,' a motto the designer deemed inappropriate for the heel.

Created with meticulous carving and veneer work, the sinuous curves and waves add drama to these statement pieces. Embued with strongly sadistic, fetishistic qualities, the shoes are injected with a great sense of humour, quirkiness and uniqueness.

These sexy silhouettes are what shoe obsessives' dreams are made of.

Within the collection is the *Azzurra* which is crafted from mahogany, sapele and ebony. This shoe is visually classical while the pair of *Dystopia* heels sculpted with a mahogany wood base, chromed bandsaw blades, aluminium, rubber and nickel spikes are more barbarous. The *Like a Virgin* shoe has a quietly erotic yet innocent quality while the staggering four foot high *Bat Girl* boots in glorious red and black vinyl represent, in my opinion, every man's sexual fantasy.

This elegant and stylish *Stilett'O'* was designed as a tribute to Perez's woodworking background. Measuring fifteen inches in height, the shoe is meticulously carved to demonstrate the beauty of the woods themselves, without further need of embellishment or frill. Rather than adding objects to the heel, Perez allows his carving to reveal the actual wood beneath the top veneer. Simple in its materials, this shoe is a study in craftsmanship and is a quiet understatement.

Perez's *Stilett'O'* shoes encompass all the qualities that we women seek when looking for innovative footwear. The spiked heel, chunky platform and quirky embellishments are a visual treat for any shoe enthusiast. However, the negative side is that we can't actually wear them! This, however, does not seem to matter as when you admire one of Perez's shoe sculptures, you instantly realize that shoes are a form of art which Perez has successfully recreated in his own idiosyncratic manner.

The layers of red and black vinyl represent not only a sexual fantasy but also symbolise surrounding a precious diva. The *Bat Girl* boot is a leading lady which Perez designed to represent high drama and theatrics. He wanted her to be the first thing you noticed when entering a room which explains why this boot measures a staggering forty-eight inches in height. Should I stare, or not? Should I touch, or not? Should I bring handcuffs, or not?

Dystopia was the first pair of Perez's shoe sculptures to be worn by a model. He built a steel rod into the shoes for added support and strength to the heel area. Even so, when the model tried to stand it became apparent that the weight distribution was not the problem, it was the stilt-like action of the height. Imagine trying to stand eighteen inches higher than yourself! For safety reasons Perez decided to have the distressed model sit for the photo shoot, as can be seen on the back cover of this book. The *Dystopia* shoes are created from a mahogany base, chromed bandsaw blades, nickel spikes, aluminium and rubber.

The idea behind *Like a Virgin* was that the heel of the shoe explores the playful domination all women have over men. Perez remarked that 'if you are "innocent" and wear white, what is your message? If you are innocent and wear "red", what is your message now?'

The accompanying cross on the heel again plays with the emotions, with the shoe itself created from snakeskin and felt, standing twenty-six inches in height.

Chapter 12

Tips for Collecting Shoes

*I*f you are thinking about building your own unique shoe collection, stick to the following tried and tested suggestions and tips and you won't go far wrong.

Only buy shoes that you love. Wear them and enjoy them and then, if they increase in value, you are onto a winner.

Look after your shoes. Before wearing them, have the shoes re-soled and re-heeled for protection and be careful not to scuff too much.

You don't have to spend a fortune. Start small by buying shoes from car boot sales, charity shops and dress agencies. You will be surprised at how cheaply you can find fantastic shoes.

Look for the most quirky, unusual and extravagant designs you can find. The more they resemble a work of art, the more likely they are to rise in value.

Italian *Bally* shoes with block heels, 1990s.

Top designer names are always worth exploring but also look at some of the high street offerings as these have just as much potential to become the collectable shoes of the future.

Buy classic designs that will never go out of fashion. These include platforms, Mary Janes, pumps and court shoes.

Heel decoration is always hot news in collecting circles so don't dismiss plain shoes that have extrovert killer heels.

Read fashion magazines such as *Grazia* and *Vogue* to see what the celebrities are wearing on their feet. If you are lucky enough to get hold of an identical pair, there is a very good chance that they will prove to be good investments.

The author, pictured with her friend Natasha, at the Jimmy Choo for H&M launch where she bought many pairs of shoes.

Buy shoes from stores that have collaborated with designers. Examples of these include the H&M collaborations with Jimmy Choo and Anna Dello Russo as well as Olivia Rubin for Dune. Since these shoes are produced in limited numbers, they possess collectable appeal.

Buy from discount outlet stores, shop sales, online retailers, pre-loved sites and internet auctions.

Display your shoe collection (when not being worn) in clear boxes on shelves and in cabinets. They were created to be admired, not hidden away from the world, as they really are fashionable works of art.

Keep your prized collection away from sunlight or extreme temperatures if you want your shoes to last forever.

Keep the original packaging. Boxes, receipts and carrier bags can add value so never throw them away. With space at a premium in most homes today, it can be tempting to clear out what might seem like 'clutter' but resist the temptation because that 'clutter' could add significantly to the value of your heels.

This, perhaps, is the most important tip of all: always wear your shoes with pride.

'You can never take too much care over the choice of your shoes. Too many women think that they are unimportant, but the real proof of an elegant woman is what is on her feet'.

Christian Dior

Acknowledgements

I have so many people to thank as each has contributed in one way or another to the writing of this book (you know who you are).

However, my special thanks go to Lisa Hooson at Pen & Sword who had probably given up thinking this book would ever be finished. Lisa, I thank you for your patience and understanding. Also, a huge thank you to my dear friend Kathy Martin for editing my book to ensure it makes sense.

My immense gratitude also goes to all the amazing people that have helped me by supplying images for the book, especially Nazim of www.shoe-icons.com who had to contend with a constant stream of emails requesting yet another of his fabulous footwear images and would reply to me even in the middle of a Saturday night.

To all the designers featured who have waited years to see their creations in print, I got there in the end and hopefully you are all happy with the result.

Huge thanks go to my close friends Trudy, Kerry, Natasha and all the mums at the school gate who have listened to me harping on about my shoe book nearly every day for the past six months.

As always, thank you, mum, for your continued support, babysitting duties and of course for initiating my love of shoes. I remember back in the 1980s prancing around in your pale blue stilettos (which I could barely walk in) when you weren't looking, longing for the day when I could wear my own pair of sky-high heels.

And finally my biggest thank you goes to Paul whom, without his constant support, I would not be able to do what I love best, and to Harry, my five year old son, who kept telling me that 'the story you are writing mummy is very long'.

Directory of Contacts

Antiques/Collectable Centres

Alfies Antique Market, 13-25 Church Street, Marylebone London, NW8 8DT, Email: info@alfiesantiques.com Tel: 0207 723 6066

Grays Antique Market, 58 Davies Street, London, W1K 5AB, Tel: 0207 629 7034

Auction Houses

Christie's Auctioneers, South Kensington, 85 Old Brompton Road, London, SW7 3LD. www.christies.com Tel: 0207 930 6074

Wellers Auctioneers, 70/70A Guildford Street, Chertsey, Surrey, KT16 9BB www.wellers-auctions.co.uk Tel: 01932 568626.

Fashion Museums

The Bath Fashion Museum, Assembly Rooms, Bennett Street, Bath, BA1 2QH www.museumofcostume.co.uk Tel: 01225 477173

The Blandford Fashion Museum, Lime Tree House, The Plocks, Blandford Forum, Dorset DT11 7AA. www.theblandfordfashionmuseum.com Tel: 01258 453006

The Bowes Museum, Barnard Castle, County Durham, DL12 8NP www.thebowes museum.org.uk Tel: 01833 637163

The Fashion and Textile Museum, 83 Bermondsey Street, London, SE1 3XF www. Ftmlondon.org Tel: 0207 407 8664

The Metropolitan Museum of Art, 1000 Fifth Avenue, New York 10028-0198 Phone: 212-535-7710 www.metmuseum.org

The Victoria and Albert Museum, Cromwell Road, London, SW7 2RL www.vam.ac.uk

Virtual Shoe Museums www.virtualshoemuseum.com

Shoe Icons www.shoe-icons.com

Stockists

Antique Dress www.antiquedress.com

Candy Says www.candysays.co.uk

Liberty of London www.libertylondon.com

Marshmallow Mountain www.marshmallowmountain.com

PaperDress Boutique www.paperdress.co.uk
Selfridges www.selfridges.com
Swank Vintage www.swankvintage.com
The Treasure Chest, 6 Thame Road, Chinnor, OX39 4QS Tel: 01844 354736

Designer Shoe Houses
Thea Cadabra www.theacadabra.com
Jimmy Choo www.jimmychoo.com
Terry De Havilland www.terrydehavilland.com
H&M www.hm.com
Irregular Choice www.irregularchoice.com
Nicholas Kirkwood www.nicholaskirkwood.com
Yves Saint Laurent www.yvessaintlaurent.co.uk
Kobi Levi www.kobilevidesign.blogspot.com
Christian Louboutin www.eu.christianlouboutin.com
Alexander McQueen www.alexandermcqueen.com
Omar Angel Perez www.omarangelperez.com
Stuart Weitzman www.eu.stuartweitzman.com
Vivienne Westwood www.viviennewestwood.co.uk

Vintage Fashion Fairs
www.frockmevintagefashion.com
www.vintagefair.co.uk
www.judysvintagefair.co.uk
www.vintagefashionfairs.com
www.ilovemarkets.co.uk

Fashion Organisation
The Vintage Fashion Guild www.vintagefashionguild.org

Other Useful Sites
Ebay (internet auction site) www.eBay.co.uk
Auction Search www.the-saleroom.com
Etsy www.Etsy.com

Photographic Credits

Antiquedress ix, 3, 16, 17, 21, 36 (below), 52, 53
Arroser 104, 109, 112, (Wikimedia commons) Creative Commons 3.0
Blahnik, Manolo 7, 75, 76, 77, 79, 80, 81, 82, 83
Brewer, Susan 57
Cadabra, Thea (all photographs by Ian Murphy) vii, 66, 67, 68, 69, 70, 71, 72, 73, 74
Candy Says 5, 38, 58, 85
Christies 98
Daderot 13 (Wikimedia commons) Creative commons CC0 1.0
De Havilland, Terry 60, 61, 62, 63, 65
FA2010 15 (Wikimedia commons) public domain
Irregular Choice 128, 129, 130, 131, 132, 134
Kosters, Annejet 151, 152, 153, 154
La Dulcie Vita 26 (above)
Lamore, Mai 10, 143, 144, 145, 147, 148, 149, 150
Levi, Kobi 11, 155, 156, 157, 159, 160
Liberty of London 127
Marshmellow Mountain 87, 95, 97, 99
Martin, Tracy 8, 46, 48, 84, 88, 89, 90, 91, 92, 93, 94, 113 (below), 126, 171
McQueen, Alexandra 117, 118, 120, 122, 123, 124
Perez, Omar Angel – Introduction 161, 162, 163, 164, 166, 167, 168
Picasa 13
Raddato, Carole 14 (Wikimedia commons) Creative Commons 2.0
Rubin, Olivia 136, 137, 138, 139, 141
Sailko 33, 36 (above) (Wikimedia commons Creative Commons 3.0
Shoe Icons (Virtual shoe museum) 6, 19, 23, 24 (above) 25, 26 (below), 30, 31, 32, 45, 47, 49, 54, 55, 56, 86, 100, 103, 106, 107, 113 (above), 115, 116, 169
Ministry of Information Photo Division Photographer 37 (Wikimedia commons) Public Domain
Thompson, Sheila 28, 34, 110 (Wikimedia commons) Creative Commons 2.0
Winston 789 111 (Wikimedia commons) Creative Commons 3.0

Index